500 Years of
OBSCENE...
and Counting...

Books by Curt Johnson

Novels
Hobbledehoy's Hero
Nobody's Perfect
Lace and a Bobbitt (novella)
The Morning Light
Song for Three Voices
Thanksgiving in Vegas (novella)

Anthologies (Ed.)
Short Stories from the Literary Magazines
  (with Jarvis Thurston)
The Best Little Magazine Fiction: 1970
The Best Little Magazine Fiction: 1971
  (with Alvin Greenberg)
Writers in Revolt: The "Anvil" Anthology
  (with Jack Conroy)

Nonfiction
How to Restore Antique and Classic Cars
  (with George Uskali)
The Forbidden Writings of Lee Wallek
Green Isle in the Sea: An Informal History of the
  Alternative Press, 1960-85 (ed. with Diane Kruchkow)
The Mafia Manager
Wicked City Chicago: From Kenna to Capone
  (with R. Craig Sautter)
Five Hundred Years of OBSCENE . . . and Counting . . .

Reference
Who's Who in Writers, Editors & Poets, biennial
  (ed., 1985-96, with Frank Nipp)

500 Years of OBSCENE...
and Counting...

Curt Johnson

december press

A special issue of December Magazine,
comprising vol. 39, no. 1, 1997

Five Hundred Years of OBSCENE . . . and Counting . . .
by Curt Johnson

ISBN 0-913204-34-X
Library of Congress Catalog Card Number: 96-086472

Cover photograph by Molly Winkelman
(*Chicago Tribune*)
"How can we know the dancer from the dance?"

Cover design by Necia Wakefield

For permission to use material from *A Place
Called Bird*, grateful acknowledgment is made
to the author, Tony Parker, and to David
Godwin Associates.

Published by December Press
Box 302, Highland Park, Illinois 60035

To Minnijean Brown, Elizabeth Eckford, Ernest Green, Thelma Mothershed, Melba Pattillo, Gloria Ray, Terrence Roberts, Jefferson Thomas, and Carlotta Walls—who in 1957-58, at Little Rock's Central High School, acting courageously on their beliefs, brought about long overdue change . . .

And for Necia, again, with love—

Ten men in our country could buy the whole
world and ten million can't buy enough to eat.
                                        —Will Rogers

Harper's creek and roarin' ribber,
Thar, my dear, we'll live forebber;
Den we'll go to de Ingin nation,
All I want in dis creation,
Is pretty little wife and big plantation.
                        —A version of the American Dream

Contents

Illustrations

National Guard troopers, white citizens of Arkansas' capital, and fellow classmates welcome Elizabeth Eckford, one of nine black students who integrated Little Rock's Central High School in 1957-58. (UPI/Corbis-Bettmann)

Preface

In 1955 the surpassing American contralto Marian Anderson was in Helsinki to appear in a concert honoring the Finnish composer Jan Sibelius on his 90th birthday. Adverse weather conditions kept the old man housebound, however, and he was unable to attend the celebration of his life's achievements.

The next day Marian Anderson traveled to Sibelius' home and there she sang all of her concert selections again, for him alone. When she finished, Sibelius went to her, took her hand and kissed it. He said, "Miss Anderson, the roof of my house is too low for you."

When Christopher Columbus was sailing the blue Caribbean in 1492, he kidnapped ten to twenty-five Arawak aborigines and took them back to Spain (only seven or eight survived the voyage). On his return to Haiti in 1493 his men set out to conquer the Arawaks, hunting them as well for sport and dog food. They enslaved 500 to labor for the Spaniards who remained in Haiti to colonize it and took 500 back to Spain (200 arriving alive). In the years that followed they would take at least 5,000 more back to Spain as slaves.

In 1499 Columbus made a major gold strike in Haiti and he and his successors then forced hundreds of thousands of the Arawaks to mine the gold for them. Before Columbus set foot in Haiti, its population is estimated to have been as high as eight million people. In 60 years this native population was wiped out, one of the first instances of genocide in human history.

During the attrition, a native chief (*cacique*) of the Arawaks gathered his people together and asked them if they knew why the

Spanish persecuted them. They replied that it was because the Spanish were cruel and bad. Bartolomé de las Casas, a Spanish adventurer and later a plantation owner and later still a priest, recorded what followed:

> "I will tell you why they do it," the *cacique* stated, "and it is this—because they have a lord whom they love very much, and I will show him to you."
>
> He held up a small basket made from palms full of gold, and he said, "Here is their lord, whom they serve and adore. . . . To have this lord, they make us suffer, for him they persecute us, for him they have killed our parents, brothers, all our people. . . . Let us not hide this lord from the Christians in any place, for even if we should hide it in our intestines, they would get it out of us; therefore let us throw it in this river, under the water, and they will not know where it is."
>
> Whereupon they threw the gold into the river.

The Spanish hunted down this *cacique* and burned him alive. Four hundred and fifty years later, the murderous instincts of the powerful remained steadfast. The 31-year-old Guatemalan poet Otto Rene Castillo—whose "Apolitical Intellectuals" appears in the "Portfolio" chapter of this book—was burned alive in 1967 after four days of torture by the Guatemalan military. The soldiers' reasons were much the same as those of the Conquistadores' troops: Castillo's words, if they led to action, would deprive their masters of gain.

Because of the steadily dwindling supply of native labor in Haiti, Columbus' son in 1505 initiated a slave trade from Africa across the Atlantic. This was the beginning of what became a brisk business in human beings. In later years the wealth of some of the most reverenced names in Yankeedom (the Lowells and the Cabots—who speak only to God—for instance) got its beginnings from this trade in human flesh. The slaves cultivated cane sugar in the Indies, from which molasses was made, from which the New England merchants made rum, which was, in turn, sold to finance slaving expeditions. From the stolen labor of slaves came much of the capital that financed the American Revolution (and the Industrial Revolution). Writing in 1775, John Adams said: "I know not why we should blush to confess that molasses was an essential ingredient in American independence."

Columbus' feats of exploitation ultimately revolutionized race relations in the world and established the dominance over the entire globe of the white European male by two means: the transatlantic slave trade (which created a black underclass in the New World), and the seizure of the land and wealth and labor of indigenous populations (which sometimes meant exterminating them). Additionally, the immense amounts of gold and silver sent back to Europe by Columbus and the Conquistadores who came after him quickened the first stirrings of modern capitalism, the economic system that soon came to govern the commercial traffic of the world.

In 1934 the long-running Broadway play *Green Pastures*, based on the novel *Old Man Adam and His Chillun* by Roark Bradford, was performed at the National Theater in Washington, D.C. Though the play had an all-Negro cast, Negroes were not allowed to buy tickets—there or at any other downtown theater in our nation's capital. Perhaps few could have afforded to attend in any case. The Depression gripped the country in 1934 and for every white of the millions out of work in the nation there were proportionately three or four blacks.

In 1939 the Daughters of the American Revolution, one of America's leading patriotic societies, barred Marian Anderson from singing at their Constitution Hall because she was black. In protest, Eleanor Roosevelt, the wife of the President, resigned her membership in the DAR.

Harold L. Ickes, President Roosevelt's Secretary of the Interior, invited Miss Anderson to give her recital on Easter Sunday from the steps of the Lincoln Memorial, which she did on that cloudy day before an audience of 75,000 people, most of them black.

Ickes introduced her. "In this great auditorium under the sky, all of us are free," he began. "When God gave us this wonderful outdoors and the sun and the moon and the stars, He made no distinction of race, creed, or color." Concluding, Ickes said, "Genius draws no color line. She has endowed Marian Anderson with such a voice as lifts any individual above his fellows and is a matter of exultant pride to any race." . . . And then Marian Anderson sang.

Thirteen years later, in 1952, at a May 20th memorial service for Ickes, who had died earlier in that year, Marian Anderson sang again at the Lincoln Memorial. Dressed in a sweeping blue taffeta gown and holding an armful of blood-red roses against her breast, she sang "Come, Sweet Death," and then, as she had in 1939, "Ave Maria" and the spirituals "Gospel Train" and "Trampin' " and, finally, together with the whole attendance of perhaps 2,500 people standing and singing with her, "America, the Beautiful."

On May 17, 1954, the U.S. Supreme Court decided that segregation in the schools of the nation must end. States' rights segregationists said they would defy that decision and school desegregation was slow in coming. In 1956 William Faulkner, Oxford, Mississippi's most famous citizen, whose novels and stories paint brooding portraits of black and white Southerners and unravel many of the reasons for the convoluted tensions between them, said that white Southerners would "accept another Civil War, knowing they're going to lose," rather than agree to immediate desegregation of their schools. If he himself were forced to make a choice, he said, he would "fight for Mississippi against the United States even if it meant going out into the streets and shooting Negroes." He said, "If there's no middle ground, if people like me have got to choose, then I'm on the side of Mississippi." Advocating a tortoise-paced gradualism, he said, "Let us sweat in our own fears for a little while."

These were the views of one of the South's most articulate, thoughtful, compassionate whites, a man who understood the evils of racial intolerance, yet for whom his home state meant only the whites in it. In Faulkner's novel *Absalom, Absalom!* Quentin Compson is asked why he hates the South, and the response has been taken to be Faulkner protesting too much for himself: " 'I don't hate it,' Quentin replied quickly. 'I don't hate it . . . I don't hate it. I don't. I don't hate it! I don't hate it!' "

The schools of Arkansas moved only slightly faster than those of other Southern states to implement the Supreme Court's desegregation decision.

After much study, Little Rock's school board proposed on May 24, 1955, the admittance of Negro students to its all-white Central High School in the fall of 1957, and this proposal was approved as "deliberate and speedy" by a federal judge. The proposal was met with reluctant acceptance by the 107,000 residents of Little Rock, 30,000 of them black, mostly underclass. The blacks, too, had their fears—but nine black children volunteered to enroll.

When the time approached for first classes, Arkansas' governor, Orval Faubus, announced on television that if Negro students attempted to enter Central High, "blood will run in the streets," a prediction he repeated in the weeks that followed. The first attempt to enter was made on September 4. Governor Faubus had called out the Arkansas National Guard to prevent the nine from entering and the Guard and troopers from the Arkansas State Police and a raging mob of white men, women, and teenagers greeted the nine and turned them away.

Three weeks later, on the Sabbath before the nine were to try a second time, many Little Rock ministers asked their congregations to take action against the impending affront to white people, to the Southern way of life, and to God. The head of Little Rock's Mothers League called for a demonstration in front of the school.

On September 23, 1957, a screaming mob of white men and women, some of them from adjoining states, gathered again in front of Central High: "Just let those niggers show up! Just let 'em try!" "Niggers go home! Niggers, go back where you belong!" The rope-carrying lynch mob's rage was so intense, its numbers so large—at least a thousand—that the Little Rock police seriously considered giving the mob one of the nine young blacks in order to save the rest.

"Let one of those kids hang? How's that gonna look? Niggers or not, they're children, and we got a job to do," said Eugene Smith, Assistant Chief of the Little Rock Police Department—and he and other Little Rock police officers that day did the job police do: they protected and they served.

In response to Governor Faubus' defiance, the federal government sent soldiers of the 101st Airborne to shield the nine Negroes from their tormentors. The President ordered the Army in only at the insistence of his Attorney General, however. The President's own inclination was to let matters take their own course. As he often pontificated, you can't legislate morality.

The 101st stayed for eight weeks of the term. The rest of the school year the nine young blacks were on their own to face—every day—constant harassment and brutal treatment from their classmates—"The niggers! Keep the niggers out!"—early on, mobs around the school armed with guns, ropes, clubs, rocks, dynamite, and every day throughout the school year, lighted balls of paper thrown at their hair, excrement thrown at them in school corridors, flying food in the school cafeteria, spitting, shin-kicking, heel-stepping, tripping. They were slammed into lockers, shoved down staircases; their street clothes were dumped into running showers during gym class; paint, ink, and urine were thrown on them, burning oil was sprayed into their faces, switch blades were pressed against their cheeks and throats. And the threat of death on the way to or from Central High was present every day—every day—should they be so incautious as to be caught isolated from others and entrapped by the ever-present roving bands of young whites.

None of the teachers or school officials at Central High helped the nine. One or two of the teachers remained brusquely neutral, though unsympathetic. If any of the nine complained, they were reprimanded and punished. If they protested to their oppressors they knew they would be suspended, as one was.

On a snowy day in February they were pelted with snowballs filled with rocks as they waited for their ride home. Little Rock police officers and members of Arkansas' federalized National Guard looked on with arms folded, unmoved and unmoving, even when the children pleaded for their assistance. This was a typical encounter for the nine young blacks, typical of each day during an entire school year.

At their homes in the night there were rocks, firebombs, and shotgun blasts from passing cars. Their families' phones rang incessantly, the callers growling and shrieking threats and vile insults. The nine were, of course, ostracized by their 1,950 white classmates from whom, like all teenagers, they needed acceptance and approval.

Try to imagine yourself 15 years old again. Imagine waking up five mornings of every week knowing that when you go to school you will face a day of physical and psychological torment and possibly death. For that matter, try to imagine yourself suppressing your fear and rage and frustration for nine days, let alone nine months.

One of the volunteers, Melba Pattillo Beals, described the events of that Little Rock year in a book published in 1994 titled *Warriors Don't Cry*:

> "Nigger," I would whisper to remind myself. That's all I am to them. They don't see me as a real person. There even came a moment when I pinched myself to see if I was really there. So many times I wanted to shout, "I'm Melba, don't you see me? I play the piano, I can make blouses, I can write poems . . . and I sing."

The events of the year Melba Pattillo Beals recounts are grotesque. It is beyond belief that the whites of Little Rock, or anywhere else, adult and teenaged, could have acted with the relentless, long-term hate and brutality and homicidal intent that they did—though we know in Nazi Germany it happened for 10 long years. It is beyond comprehension that the nine black children were able to withstand the unremitting cruelty that expressed that hate.

Little Rock's Central High School is a tall and majestic building, seven stories high and stretching over two long city blocks. It could be twice as tall and imposing as it is and its roof would still be too low for the nine black children who walked its halls that first year of integration.

The history books will record that Southern schools were integrated during Dwight D. Eisenhower's Presidency. But Dwight David Eisenhower had virtually nothing to do with it. He dispatched the 101st Airborne to Little Rock only because his Attorney General, Herbert Brownell, Jr., told him he must. When Brownell offered his resignation later in 1957, Eisenhower accepted it; Brownell was far too pro-integration to suit the President.

In 1956 Eisenhower had won reelection by a plurality of 9,549,681 votes, one and a half times the figures of his decisive victory four years before. His vote total was 35,581,003. His popularity was never higher. Supreme commander of Allied forces in their victory over Nazi Germany in World War II, a five-star General of the Army, acknowledged to be the world's greatest living soldier, revered and idolized by his countrymen, all Dwight Eisenhower had to do in 1957 to restore order to Little Rock and to snuff out Governor Faubus' defiance of the law of the land was to take his prestige and presence to Central High School and stand in its main entrance as the nine black children entered.

But Dwight David Eisenhower did nothing. The nation's heroic leader, who had sworn to uphold and defend the Constitution, was indifferent to the firestorm of civil rights that was Little Rock and to the daily pain and suffering of nine black children. When all was said and done, and not done, Eisenhower was no better than the worst white among us.

The South did not, of course, accede gracefully after Little Rock. In 1960 the writer John Steinbeck was in New Orleans when a school there was in the protracted process of being integrated. One cold morning he observed what happened at the school and in his *Travels with Charley* he reported on that morning:

> Across the street from the school the police had set up wooden barriers to keep the crowd back, and they paraded back and forth, ignoring the jokes called to them. The front of the school was deserted but along the curb United States Marshals were spaced, not in uniform but wearing armbands to identify them. . . .
>
> It was apparent where the Cheerleaders were, because people shoved forward to try to get near them. They had a favored place at the barricade directly across from the school

entrance, and in that area a concentration of police stamped their feet and slapped their hands together in unaccustomed gloves.

The "Cheerleaders" were a group of women—white women—who gathered in front of the school every morning before school opened and again every afternoon when school let out.

The show opened on time. Sound of sirens. Motorcycle cops. Then two big black cars filled with big men in blond felt hats pulled up in front of the school. The crowd seemed to hold its breath. Four big marshals got out of each car and from somewhere in the automobiles they extracted the littlest Negro girl you ever saw, dressed in shining starchy white, with new white shoes on feet so little they were almost round. Her face and little legs were very black against the white.

The big marshals stood her on the curb and a jangle of jeering shrieks went up from behind the barricades. The little girl did not look at the howling crowd but from the side the whites of her eyes showed like those of a frightened fawn. The men turned her around like a doll, and then the strange procession moved up the broad walk toward the school, and the child was even more a mite because the men were so big. Then the girl made a curious hop, and I think I know what it was. I think in her whole life she had not gone ten steps without skipping, but now in the middle of her first skip the weight bore her down and her little round feet took measured, reluctant steps between the tall guards. Slowly they climbed the steps and entered the school. . . .

A shrill, grating voice rang out. The yelling was not in chorus. Each took a turn and at the end of each the crowd broke into howls and roars and whistles of applause. This is what they had come to see and hear.

No newspaper had printed the words these women shouted. . . . On television the sound track was made to blur or had crowd noises cut in to cover. But now I heard the words, bestial and filthy and degenerate. . . .

. . . But there was something far worse here than dirt, a kind of frightening witches' Sabbath. . . .

. . . These blowzy women with their little hats and their clippings hungered for attention. They wanted to be admired. They simpered in happy, almost innocent triumph when they were applauded. Theirs was the demented cruelty of egocentric children, and somehow this made their insensate beastliness much more heartbreaking. . .

The crowd behind the barrier roared and cheered and pounded one another with joy. . . .

. . . I knew New Orleans, I have over the years had many friends there, thoughtful, gentle people, with a tradition of kindness and courtesy. . . . How many days I have spent with Roark Bradford, who took Louisiana sounds and sights and created God and the Green Pastures to which He leadeth us. I looked in the crowd for such faces of such people and they were not there. . . . [Where were] the ones whose arms would ache to gather up the small scared black mite?

I don't know where they were. Perhaps they felt as helpless as I did, but they left New Orleans misrepresented to the world. The crowd, no doubt, rushed home to see themselves on television, and what they saw went out all over the world, unchallenged by the other things I know are there.

All this and more was working at the back of my mind when I began this book early in 1996. I knew that race relations between whites and blacks had changed greatly in my lifetime, for the better, so it was said, yet something felt wrong. As I finished writing this book the KKK-airheads in the country had begun to burn and vandalize black churches, anti-Semitism was increasing and prejudice against Latinos was increasing. It was also becoming clear that the parlor liberals of the country had grown weary of (or bored with) trying to solve the race problem, while the archest of our conservatives wanted to solve the race problem by putting all black males in prison and starving their wives, sweethearts, and children. Race relations in the United States seemed in 1996 to be back where they were in 1896—a low point in black history— and I could only thank my lucky stars I had been born white. More, the poor and homeless were becoming pariahs to the middle class (they have always been pariahs to the overclass).

I attempted to discover a reason or reasons for what was happening, to decipher the runes. Here I will only say that considering the renewal of hatred in the United States as we approach the millennium, perhaps it would be well for us to recall what James Baldwin wrote in 1955: "Hatred, which could destroy so much, never failed to destroy the man who hated and this was an immutable law."

One day while I was working on this book my son (the only lawyer I completely trust) asked me what it was about. "Racism and capitalism," I answered.

"Oh, more light reading, huh?" he said. . . . Thanks a lot, Mark.

My thanks also to Necia Tesla Wakefield for her help and encouragement while this book was being written and for her admonition to "Tell the truth and shame the devil"; to Florence Hamlish Levinsohn for her support and expert and substantive counsel; to Harlan N. Olafson, formerly political editor of *December* magazine and my oldest and best friend, for not offering advice; to Phyllis Magida, as always; to Kathryn E. King, as always; and especially to Diane Kruchkow, as always; and to Betty Fox and her husband Ira Rosenberg, who are friends in deed. If I could think of one reason in the world to thank the quickest wit in the West, the Prez of Club d'Ronde, the panjandrum of Park Ridge, and long-time Caxton Club member Tom Legge for his help on this book, I'd do it.

For their generous permission to use the material found in the "Nicodemus" chapter from the book *A Place Called Bird*, I would like to thank *Bird*'s author, Tony Parker, and David Godwin Associates. An 87-year-old black matriarch who lived in Nicodemus, outside of Bird, had this to say when Tony Parker interviewed her in the late 1980s, and I will close this Preface with her words about her hopes for America, the beautiful:

> What I want for America is what I've wanted all my long life, and that's peace, not war, and love, not hate. I want to see my country at peace with every other country in the world, all living together in peace and all one big family, which is what they are. And in my country I want all people to live together in love as one big family too: black and white, yellow and brown, everyone together. The Lord didn't make us all to be quarrelling and bickering with one another, he made us as His children to help one another. America, this is a big country with a big heart and millions of decent folk who've done a whole lot of things they can be proud of, like freedom and emancipation and such things as that. So sure, let's be proud of ourselves: but proud for the right things, not proud because we can win wars, there's nothing in that to be proud of. To be peaceful and gentle and kind, that's what we should be proud of.

Far, Far Away

Toward the close of the Civil War an ex-slave who had joined the Union Army found his former master among the Confederate prisoners he was guarding. "Hello, massa!" he said delightedly, "bottom rail top dis time!"

As a student at the State University of Iowa in Iowa City 90 years later, one of the courses I took was "The Negro in America," given by Professor George R. Ragland, Jr., a big, quiet-spoken instructor in the department of sociology and anthropology. He was shooting for his Ph.D. degree.

Our main assigned text was Maurice R. Davie's *Negroes in American Society.* We also read in Herskovits' *The Myth of the Negro Past,* Reddings' *They Came in Chains,* Ottley's *Black Odyssey,* Gunnar Myrdal's *An American Dilemma,* and half a dozen other studies, as well as the weekly newspapers the *Chicago Defender* and the Negro press bellwether, the *Pittsburgh Courier.*

At that time, 1951-52, the U.S. Senate was controlled by Southerners who, by virtue of the Senate's seniority system and the South's election laws, headed most of the important committees. In 1944, as World War II drew toward its climax, the long-prevailing attitude of Southern congressmen toward Negroes had been judiciously re-expressed by Senator James Eastland of Mississippi: "I have no prejudice in my heart, but the white race is the superior race and the Negro race an inferior race and the races must be kept separate."

From what I had seen, they were. I grew up among the Scandinavians and Germans of south-side Minneapolis; there were only two or three blacks in the grade school I went to. In high school in a small town in north-central Iowa there was only one black in our student body, Jim Sheehy, tough, fast and small. Opposing defensemen in football brought him down, when they could, in piling-on waves, shouting "Kill that nigger!" This seemed a battle cry appropriate to the occasion, if

1

somewhat lacking in the spirit of sportsmanship, because for three years Sheehy made them nervous with his speed and elusiveness. Like myself and the rest of our team, our opponents were all big, dumb, slow Nordics.

In my Navy boot-camp training company, comprised half of pale, bulky teenagers from Minnesota and Iowa and half of big, tanned teenagers from Louisiana and Texas, the apprentice seamen from the South often expressed the fullness of their hearts more forcefully and profanely than Senator Eastland had. There were no blacks in Company 251, very few on the base, but their presence in the world at large was an irritant obsessively on the minds of the boys from the bayous and the Alamo.

The term "redneck" had a more restricted meaning in that boot-camp company in 1946; it was something you got, not what you were. It meant to become angry. If a Texan wanted to forestall someone's anger, he would say, "Hey now, don't you get the redneck!" (The thought of blacks co-existing gave Southerners the redneck, for example.) There seems an obvious connection between that time's limited meaning of the term and its present-day more general usage as a noun defining a type and, usually, a class.

On Uncle Sam's U.S.S. *Askari* (ARL 30) I saw that Negroes were isolated, also, serving exclusively as waiters in the officers' mess. That they were good at this task could not be denied, just as in civilian life they were acknowledged to be excellent Pullman porters. They must have liked the work, too, or they wouldn't have gravitated to it, would they. Would they?

Professor Ragland did not ever display any signs of getting the redneck—that wouldn't have been professorial—but the tenor and substance of his lectures and his understated comments during class discussions indicated, I thought, a deep, pessimistic disgust with the situation of blacks in the United States. And I remember he shocked our class one day by stating that Abraham Lincoln had not always been the staunch friend of the Negro he was made out to be.

For myself, I felt certain that given good will and education, knowledge and wisdom, such as were getting at the University in Iowa City (which styled itself, naturally, "The Athens of the Midwest"), the Negro problem in the United States would eventually resolve itself and we could all of us live side by side in a peaceable kingdom—and sooner rather than later. If prejudice was learned, it stood to reason it could be unlearned.

The disparity between Professor Ragland's pessimism and my own optimism, I felt, was probably most due to the fact that I was 10 years younger than he was—and possibly to the fact that he was black.

That spring I got a degree and on graduation day had a few

2

celebratory beers with Ollie Cox, a Negro, who had also gotten a degree that day. We knew each other from having worked together on the campus humor magazine. (One of Ollie's talents was that he could talk scat, a gift that fascinated our leader, Nick Thimmesch—who later became a nationally syndicated journalist; conservative, as it happened, which was strange, given his collegiate self.)

Ollie and I congratulated each other and I said, "Feels pretty good, huh?"

Ollie looked back at me almost grimly.

"What's the matter?" I asked. "You've got your master's. Smile!"

He sipped at his beer and finally he said, "Sure." Then he laughed. "You know any tiny, black, backwater schools?"

What I did not learn in Professor Ragland's class and didn't find out about until much later was that all the years I had been at Iowa a black student who needed a haircut had to travel across the river to Cedar Rapids to get it, a distance of 50 or so miles. . . . That would have included Professor Ragland, too, wouldn't it.

In 1865, by the accidents of war, the bottom rail had been briefly on top, yes, but only very briefly. Ninety years later it was and had been for a long time before bottom rail again, both north and south.

For the wealthy in this country that situation was an ongoing economic lever and boon. For the much more numerous redneck population it was a psychological necessity.

In the 1960s the black leader Malcolm X had a sure-fire laugh-provoker in his speeches:

Question: What is a black man with a Ph.D.?

Answer: A nigger.

3

Immigrant Italian railroad workers near Butte, Montana, 1904.
(University of Illinois at Chicago, The University Library, Dept. of
Special Collections, Italian-American Collection)

The Gilded Age

Clear across the country in the mid- and late 19th century the U.S. Congress gave the railroad tycoons of the nation not only cash grants to build west but also every other section (640 acres each) on either side of the right-of-way. To lay track in the Midwest and across the grassy plains, however, all you had to do was drop and space the ties, slap down rail, and spike in. Easier going would have been hard to find; no very great inducements should have been necessary. The hundreds of millions of dollars and alternate sections of hundreds of thousands of acres of rich public land were an outright gift from all of the people of the United States to only a relatively few of their more cunning and grasping fellow citizens.

The end of the Civil War ushered in a time of great commercial and industrial growth in the victorious North. Mark Twain and Charles Dudley Warner collaborated to write a novel about this era, *The Gilded Age*, which satirically chronicled the corruption of the nation's political process as a compliant Congress parceled out the continent's resources to the highest bidders.

Here is a small railroad contractor in *The Gilded Age* musing on how the government's largesse was going to benefit him:

"... Brown and Schaick have, or will have, the control for the whole line of the Salt Lick Pacific Extension, forty thousand dollars a mile over the prairie, with extra for hardpan—and it'll be pretty much all hardpan I can tell you; besides every alternate section of land on this line. There's millions in the job. I'm to have the subcontract for the first fifty miles, and you can bet it's a soft thing."

"I'll tell you what you do, Philip," continued Harry, in a burst of generosity, "if I don't get you into my contract, you'll be with the engineers, and you just stick a stake at the first

5

ground marked for a depot, buy the land of the farmer before he knows where the depot will be, and we'll turn a hundred or so on that. I'll advance the money for the payments, and you can sell the lots. . . ."

And here a larger contractor, but musing, too, on prospects of future wealth:

"We'll buy the lands," explained he, "on long time, backed by the notes of good men; and then mortgage them for money enough to get the road well on. Then get the towns on the line to issue their bonds for stock, and sell their bonds for enough to complete the road, and partly stock it, especially if we mortgage each section as we complete it. We can then sell the rest of the stock on the prospect of the business of the road through an improved country, and also sell the lands at a big advance, on the strength of the road. All we want," continued Mr. Bigler in his frank manner, "is a few thousand dollars to start the surveys, and arrange things in the legislature. There is some parties will have to be seen, who might make us trouble."

The contractor continues in this vein until a young lady at the dining table interrupts him with: " 'Well, what would become of the poor people who had been led to put their little money into the speculation, when you got out of it and left it half way?' "

Unembarrassed, but annoyed, the contractor replies:

"Why yes, Miss, of course, in a great enterprise for the benefit of the community there will little things occur, which, which—and, of course, the poor ought to be looked to; I tell my wife, that the poor must *be* looked to; if you can tell who are poor—there's so many impostors. And then, there's so many poor in the legislature to be looked after," said the contractor with a sort of a chuckle. . . .

But it was not alone in railroads that speculation and bribery flourished in post-bellum America. Anything that could be turned to a profit was. The great wealth of many U.S. families was established in the Gilded Age and we have with us today thousands of jet-setters and sun-baskers who owe their prominence in the elite of high society and their fast-lane lives of frantic leisure to forebears who schemed, worked, bilked, and bribed in that long-gone era. A great many of these descendants are jaded, nonproductive drones, male and female, but their trust funds keep right on keeping on.

You can read about the fortunes amassed in our earlier history in

Matthew Josephson's *The Robber Barons*, or Gustavus Myers' *History of the Great American Fortunes*. Ferdinand Lundberg brought these chronicles of great family wealth to the '70s and '80s of the 20th century with *America's Sixty* Families and *The Rich and the Super-Rich*.

Each of these historical resumes makes clear something our history and civics schoolbooks do not mention: The great, preponderant majority of us are not players and never will be. We have never been more than workers—easily disposable, easily replaced. Our work lives are owned by others. We are losers in the game of getting.

Two generalizations can safely be made about those who own our labor: (1) They are rich, and (2) they are white (and probably Anglo-Saxon Protestant). We can also be sure of one thing more: Our owners are not going to give up any portion of what they have or of the control it gives them of our lives—and, thus, their own—simply because they are asked to in the name of fairness.

In the 1930s the American writer F. Scott Fitzgerald remarked to his fellow writer Ernest Hemingway that the rich were different than the rest of us. Hemingway is supposed to have replied, "Yes—they have more money," a wise-ass response but considered then and now a justified putdown of Fitzgerald's naivete.

Fitzgerald, however, was seeking to understand something he both feared and envied and he finally came up with a more considered response than Hemingway's. "Let me tell you about the rich," Fitzgerald wrote. "They are different from you and me. They possess and enjoy early, and it does something to them, makes them soft where we are hard, and cynical where we are trustful, in a way that, unless you were born rich, it is difficult to understand. They think, deep in their hearts, that they are better than we are because we had to discover the compensations and refuges of life for ourselves. Even when they enter deep into our world or sink below us, they still think that they are better than we are. They are different."

So they are, and there's no tea for that fever.

Photos by Molly Winkelman

Race Relations

Dixieland Southerners believe that *any* white man is better than *every* black man. Consequently, the white man's floor must be the Negro's ceiling. If this caste order is not strictly observed, all hell is likely to break loose. This I learned at the State University of Iowa in 1952.

My notes for my "Negro in America" course that year tell me that I also learned that in American society at large, whites expect Negroes to view everything as Negroes—and so do Negroes. Thus, the Negro genius is imprisoned in the Negro problem. The Negro can live and earn his reputation only in the backwash of discrimination (that is, the unequal treatment of equals, usually by the imposition of burdens). The Negro is not permitted to go into the main current of the river itself.

The United States of America is a white man's nation and the Negro problem in America is in fact the white problem in America.

Amalgamation (the biological fusion of diverse racial stocks) is denied to the Negro, while available, as a long-run process, to other minorities. The white man discriminates against the Negro in all spheres in order to prevent miscegenation—that is, in order to maintain "race purity." The doctrine of Negro inferiority demands that the white race keep itself pure.

It is not only hard-core Southerners who truly believe that every white man is better than any black man, but overtly or covertly every white man in the United States believes this, too. Every white woman as well, and at least as devoutly as the men.

The American dilemma is that this country's whites hold two sets of beliefs: (1) that Negroes are inferior; and (2) that all men are created equal.

To reconcile these conflicting beliefs, whites must assign characteristics to Negroes that exclude them from the category "all men." Therefore, they define Negroes as a different and inferior species

9

and this definition becomes fact for many people and provides an excuse for inequality—otherwise known as *racism*, the doctrine that dictates our country's race caste system.

Racism holds that race determines the psychological abilities and cultural traits of the individual and group, that it is the primary determinant of differences between people. It also holds that the races are unequal and that the dominant race is the superior race, and that the crossing of races is biologically harmful.

I already knew this. I had a great-uncle in Mason City, Iowa, Uncle Albert, who explained it to me before I was eight years old, back in the mid-'30s. He was a railroad section foreman and by virtue of holding such a prestigious job during the Depression was a dominating presence in the family.

Hunkered down, his back against the living room couch, a cup of coffee nestled in his big-knuckled hands, my Uncle Albert declaimed against Joe Louis, the Brown Bomber, who was punching holes through the heavyweight division at that time. My uncle pointed out that this was manifestly unfair: Louis shouldn't even be permitted in the same ring as a white man.

"If you had a mule," my uncle declared in a tone that brooked no contradiction—certainly not from me—"no matter how fast he could run, they wouldn't let you enter him in the Kentucky Derby, would they?"

Prejudice is a social attitude. Prejudice is learned. (Psychologists and sociologists are of the opinion that until shortly before puberty children ordinarily lack race—and class—consciousness. My own experience runs counter to this.) A prejudiced person is for or against something or someone without empirical investigation or in open disregard of evidence. Prejudice is a resistance of the social order to change. It often seems to arise not so much when economic status is threatened but when social status is. Southern whites are prejudiced against the Negro. In the North, in addition to a variant form of this prejudice (or sometimes, though very rarely, its absence), there is racial antipathy, which is more elementary and thus more insidious.

Before the Civil War the highest prestige in the South was accorded to those who owned a landed estate—a plantation—and many slaves. The planter made the law for the plantation and its slaves; his overseer enforced that law. The very largest plantations were like small, model villages.

Slaves were the ultimate criterion of prestige and wealth in the Old South, the stamp of untitled nobility. The more slaves you owned, the higher your rank in the peerage. The landed aristocracy of the South before the Civil War amounted to no more than 3 percent of the white population. The remaining 97 percent of the white population had the

10

satisfaction of knowing that each of them, no matter how dirt-poor, was superior to *any* Negro.

Christians outnumber all other religious groups in the United States. Like the American creed of equality of all men, the Christian religion is not compatible with the race caste pattern of America. Theoretically. But the Christian religion—put your faith and hopes in Masser Jesus!—is a very good religion for slaveowners to permit their plantation slaves.

The quarrel between the North and the South in the 19th century had an economic basis, and the Civil War was fought for economic reasons—but if there had been no slaves, there would have been no war.

Emancipation freed the Negro physically but left him economically helpless in a hostile environment. In their effort to re-establish the Old South in the post-bellum South, white Southerners clung to a rationale justifying their superior status, the main tenet of which was as before: The Negro is inherently inferior—not only morally, but also as a worker and as a consumer. In fact, the rationale went, it was God's will that Negroes have a low income. Furthermore, Negroes are accustomed to living on less than whites and are satisfied with less than whites. If, God forbid, Negroes should ever attain economic equality, they might then strive for social equality, as well, and then the heavens would surely fall and all hell would surely break loose—including, possibly, intermarriage! (Curiously, the antebellum South was quite tolerant of unsanctified unions between white men and black women.)

The foregoing notes from my 1952 class "Negro in America" are at this writing 45 years old—and the more things change the more they roughly remain the same.

For the past 20 or 30 years I have watched on TV now and again the running of the eighth race at Churchill Downs on Kentucky Derby Day. While I have seen quite a few dogs break from the starting gate, never a mule. My gandydancer uncle Albert was right in his implicit answer, but he had asked the wrong question. In 1911, it was black *jockeys* who had been banned from the Derby because they'd won 15 of the first 28.

Philip Danforth Armour (1832-1901)
(Dictionary of American Portraits)

Marshall Field (1834-1906)
(Library of Congress)

Imponderables

The older I get the more I am puzzled by seemingly inexplicable mysteries. For example, if all over the world people are starving to death, why doesn't the United States feed them from its gigantic agricultural surpluses?

Or why do pro-lifers on the question of abortion sometimes feel that it would be well to murder those who are pro-choice?

Or, since Christians believe that Jesus, a Jew, is the greatest man who has ever lived, how is it that Christians almost uniformly denigrate and insult Jews?

Or, if all of mankind originated in black Africa, as most scientists who have studied the matter believe, how can the white race, whose every gene comes from black ancestors, regard the black as inferior?

Every once in a great while I have asked people I knew pretty well why such matters were. If my question was not laughed at outright, I was usually told that in time I would understand. Well, time is running out, and so far I haven't. Not very much, anyway.

The DuPonts, the Rockefellers, the Mellons, the Fords are perhaps the most well-known of America's super-rich families, but here in Chicago we have had a few—the McCormicks, the Armours, the Fields, among others.

Cyrus Hall McCormick came to Chicago from Virginia with $60 in his pocket, established a factory to manufacture a mechanical reaper and within a few years was a millionaire. His reaper played a major role in achieving the North's victory in the Civil War: Its mechanical efficiency on the table-flat farm lands of the Middle West did the work of half a million men away in uniform.

McCormick was given to fits of long-lasting temper, once taking a suit for a disputed charge of $8.70 all the way to the Supreme Court, where he won after 18 years of litigation. He worked his employees long and hard and at low wages and was angered when they were so

13

ungrateful as to ask for higher pay. He died in 1884, leaving a fortune of $10,000,000 to his heirs. Much of this fortune had been gained through investments in real estate.

Philip Danforth Armour, head of one of the world's largest meat-packing firms, came to Chicago from New York via Milwaukee in 1875. His workers lived in Chicago's Packingtown—a jungle that sprang up around the 345-acre Union stockyards where, because of Armour's low wage scale, the workers' children had to scavenge food for their families from the garbage dumps.

Armour accumulated much of his fortune trading in commodities. One of his forays into the Board of Trade pits drove the price of wheat so high that in Europe the poor could not afford bread. He died in 1901, leaving a fortune of $31,000,000.

The rapaciousness with which the founders of the great American family fortunes went after wealth was sanctioned by the country's accepted way of doing business—that is, through our country's economic religion, capitalism. A standard encyclopedia entry for "Capitalism" defines it as "the economic system characterized chiefly by the relatively few who by their ownership of capital, control most of the production, distribution, and credit. . . . Capitalism stresses the individual's freedom to undertake any enterprise, at his own risk, and in his own manner." It "has the sole aim of increasing private profits." In other words, capitalism is greed writ large, and anything goes.

The most prominent early Chicago capitalist, the merchant prince Marshall Field, came to Chicago from Massachusetts in 1856 at the age of 21 to clerk in a dry goods store for $400 a year, half of which salary he saved. In 1865 he and a partner bought out Field's employer and the store became Marshall Field and Company.

A journalist of the time reported that "When Marshall Field opened any new department, say of cutlery or hardware or millinery, jewelry, etc., or what not, he would run it at cut rates so as to give him command of the field, contenting himself with the profits of other departments. Against such a power, so concentrated against . . . the competitor, nothing could stand. . . ."

Still, like McCormick's fortune, a great part of the wealth Field amassed in his lifetime came from investments in real estate. Both Field and McCormick, of course, and Armour, too, through the accident of occupying strategic positions in a burgeoning economy, had acquired the capital to indulge in speculation on a grand scale. The overwhelming mass of U.S. population did not have this advantage. They worked for Field, Armour, and McCormick.

A short man with ice-cold, pale blue eyes, Field held a dinner at his home each year during the Christmas holidays at the end of which, over brandy and cigars, he would announce to the assembled officers of

14

his firm that among them was one who had not measured up over the past 12 months and would no longer, as of that moment, be part of their company. From such glimpses of Field's personality, an observer might infer that Marshall Field was a little sweetheart of a son of a bitch. His public actions seconded that notion.

In 1877 Field volunteered his store's fleet of delivery wagons to transport Chicago policemen from one troubled area of the city to another to put down a strike effort by railroad workers. The next year he, McCormick, Armour and other church-going Board of Trade members subscribed secretly to arm the Illinois National Guard with Gatling guns in preparation for "what danger if any was to be anticipated from the communistic element in the city."

On May 4, 1886, at dusk, during a meeting of workers at Haymarket Square in Chicago to protest police tactics against strikers at the McCormick-Harvester plant, a bomb was thrown.

The police opened fire and a patrolman and six workers were killed, 200 wounded. Eight men were arbitrarily selected for arrest—two of whom had not even been at Haymarket Square that evening.

Marshall Field went to City Hall and demanded of the mayor that he repress free speech in the interests of public safety. About the police action in Haymarket Square, Field said, "The police have acted nobly and deserve the highest commendation of all citizens." It was rumored that he was holding secret conferences with other business leaders to ensure that the eight accused were hanged.

The person who threw the bomb—for all anyone knows, it was a policeman—was never identified but the eight who had been selected for trial were found guilty.

The governor of Illinois was willing to commute the sentences of the condemned provided that the civic leaders of Chicago approved. Fifty upright men of commerce gathered for an extralegal life-and-death hearing and Marshall Field introduced his chosen spokesman, the State's Attorney, who argued that those who roused the rabble deserved death. The 50 then cast their votes.

The man who had called the meeting for the governor and spoken for clemency said, "Afterwards many of the men present came around to see me singly and said they . . . would have been glad to join me . . . but that in the face of the opposition of powerful men like Marshall Field they did not like to do so, as it might injure them in business or socially."

On November 11, 1887, four of the eight were hanged, a fifth having already killed himself in his cell. Marshall Field died 19 years later, in 1906, leaving a fortune of $120,000,000, most of it to his two grandsons under terms that made it probable that their shares would grow to $300,000,000 in their lifetimes.

Why would the richest, most respected capitalist in the city of Chicago cold-bloodedly bend his every effort and energy to see that men he did not even know were put to death?

It is easier to understand the meatpacker Armour than Marshall Field. When asked late in his life why he did not retire, since he had far more money than anyone would know what to do with, Armour replied, "Because I have no other interest in life than my business. . . . I do not love the money; what I do love is the getting of it."

Perhaps that answer explains Field, as well. Perhaps. But it is difficult to forget the poor in Europe starving for bread because of Armour's love of money—the getting of it—or the children in Packingtown scavenging garbage dumps for food. Armour's recreation was not exactly harmless. Very little the very rich do is. Ask the five men who were condemned and died for Haymarket.

The Road Isn't Easy

The nationalities, the ethnic groups (the tribes and their mixtures from prehistory) that came to this country from Europe, came because they believed that if they worked hard here they could find decent livings for themselves and their families and that their children would have an opportunity for better lives than their own. They came to live the American Dream.

Beginning in 1619, when 20 blacks were brought to this continent in chains and shackles on a Dutch man-of-war, British-manned, Africans were taken by slavers from whatever freedom—not always that much—they had enjoyed in their homelands and doomed to a life here of involuntary servitude, generation after generation after generation. They were snatched from their tribes by raiders from other tribes and marched to the slavers at coastal trading centers. They were not immigrants; they did not come here of their own free will. (Many, many blacks in this country today have lineages that go back well beyond the arrivals of the forebears of many whites. Well beyond 1776, in case the Daughters of the American Revolution are keeping records.)

For the Negro sold off the auction block in this country, tomorrow was going to be lived like today, which was lived like yesterday: working for the Man—they were his property. Besides the greater proportion of melanin in their skin, the chief feature that distinguished the black from the white in North America was that the white could hope. Men live on hope, even if they die in despair. In the Old South of King Cotton, the black man could muster no hope—except for another, better life with Jesus. The black's lot in this world was despair, a lifetime of it. And the despair of perpetual bondage was the only legacy the slave bequeathed his children.

What condemned the Negro to such wretchedness, to a lifetime of helpless rage and unimaginable frustration? Simple: The slave was cheap labor.

17

But enslavement had to be justified, and so it was, by beliefs held by whites that marked the Negro as different and inferior. Among these were (1) the belief that the Negro was child-like and could adjust easily, even happily. to social situations (such as slavery) that whites would find intolerable; (2) that only the poorest stock of Africa was enslaved; (3) that the Negroes brought to North America had no common culture because they came from widely separated places in the continent of Africa; and (4) that the culture of Africa was, at best, the culture of savages.

The earth is flat, the moon is made of green cheese, the Brooklyn Bridge is for sale—cheap—and the Holocaust never happened: equally valid beliefs. In Africa the Negro had over millennia developed sophisticated, intricate social systems; the handicaps imposed on him in the New World, however, destroyed these systems. Further, there was no selection of slaves so as to take only the poorest (but even if the poorest could be determined, how did that justify slavery?); slaves were levied en masse. Neither were they drawn from widely scattered locations in Africa; black raiders and slavers took their victims from West Africa—Dahomey, the Ivory Coast, Ghana, Nigeria—sometimes the Congo or Gambia. Finally, to say that one culture is savage compared to another is to use discredited ethnology.

When I was a small boy, six or so, and had not yet come into close contact with Negroes, an older boy assured me that Negroes had a distinct smell all their own. A few days later I was seated in a grade-school assembly behind a Negro boy. I eased forward and sniffed.

Sure enough, Negroes did have a smell unlike us white folks, sure enough!

As far as the lack of a common culture is concerned, Negroes brought to North America were stripped of whatever commonalities they may have shared in Africa. Here they were property, like the hogs the master owned, his sheep, his poultry. They were not humans, they were chattel, and chattel has no culturally shared past. Indeed, for purposes of apportioning the congressional representation of states, the U.S. Constitution, our country's most revered political text, calculated slaves as worth only three-fifths of a free person, but without their own vote, of course.

The myth of the Negro based on the beliefs held in the Old South to justify slavery overspread all of the states and exists in an adulterated form today, almost four centuries after it had its beginnings. If you are white, ask yourself if you don't deep down believe at least some of the following: that blacks are of a child-like nature; that they adjust more easily than whites to straitened circumstances, that is, are cheerful, even happy, most of the time, no matter what; that blacks have great physical strength and athletic ability but are lazy; and that they are not quite as

18

bright as whites. *All* blacks, that is.

We generally perceive what we preconceive. We find what we are searching for, even when it is not there. Ten years passed before I was again physically close enough to a Negro to be aware of the unusual odor peculiar to his blackness, if blacks had such an odor. They didn't—he didn't—nor has any since.

But if you are white, confess it: All blacks have an innate, natural sense of rhythm, don't they; and as a result, are fantastically good musicians, and singers, and dancers. And white women find black men very sexually attractive, don't they (but of course black men are phenomenally well-endowed). And all black women are wildly exotic creatures, passionate, always willing, and insatiable lovers, am I right? Or am I wrong?

The slave plantation of the Old South forced the Negro to learn a new language and to abandon the social systems he had lived in. It destroyed his African pattern of family life, whatever it may have been. It destroyed his African economic system, his African political institutions, and his African religious beliefs. Thus, Negroes as slaves became a people with only a remnant of a culture of their own, a people without a past.

On March 6, 1857, U.S. Supreme Court Chief Justice Roger B. Taney rendered the majority opinion in the case of *Dred Scott v. Sandford*. The majority of the court declared against Scott's claim to freedom on three grounds: (1) Since he was a Negro, he could not be a U.S. citizen and thus could not sue in federal court; (2) since he was a resident of Missouri, the laws of Illinois (a free state), where he had been a resident, did not pertain to him; and (3) the Missouri Compromise of 1820, which had forbidden slavery north of latitude 36° 31' (the Mason-Dixon Line), was unconstitutional, anyway, since it deprived citizens of property (slaves) without due process of law. The decision proclaimed that "a Negro had no rights a white man was bound to respect."

So Dred Scott was restored to his owner and four years later, in 1861, the states went to war against one another, and after four years of blood and agony the boys in blue overcame the boys in grey. The Union was preserved, but without slavery. The 13th Amendment confirmed this in 1865.

An ex-slave, a freedman, from Mississippi recalled his feelings: "I was right smart bit by de freedom bug for awhile. It sounded pow'ful nice to be tol: 'You don't have to chop cotton no more. You can th'ow dat hoe down an' go fishin' whensoever de notion strikes you. An' you can roam 'roun' at night an court gals jus' as you please.' Aint no marster gwine a-say to you, 'Charlie, you's got to be back when de clock strikes nine.' I was fool 'nough to b'lieve all dat kin' o' stuff."

On Good Friday April 14, 1865, five days after Lee's surrender

19

to Grant at Appomattox, President Lincoln was shot. He died a little before 7:30 the next morning, as a week before he had dreamed he would. A witness described this scene in Washington, D.C.: "On the Avenue in front of the White House were several hundred colored people, mostly women and children, weeping and wailing their loss. This crowd did not appear to diminish through the whole of that cold, wet day; they seemed not to know what was to be their fate since their great benefactor was dead, and their hopeless grief affected me more than almost anything else, though strong and brave men wept when I met them."

Lincoln had said, "As I would not be a *slave*, so I would not be a *master*. This expresses my idea of democracy—Whatever differs from this, to the extent of the difference, is no democracy." Most of the victorious North wanted to believe that they felt this way, too—so long as it cost them no more than some tears.

"Oh sometimes it causes me to tremble—tremble—tremble.
Were you there when they crucified my Lord?"

A Model Capitalist

George Mortimer Pullman was born in Brocton, New York, in 1831 and came to Chicago in 1855 with a background as a construction engineer and cabinetmaker. He supervised the lifting of many of Chicago's downtown buildings out of the mud, then developed the first railway sleeping car suitable for long-distance travel, then the dining car, then the parlor car. In 1867 he organized the Pullman Palace Car Company. In 1880 he built a factory south of Chicago and around it the model town of Pullman, Illinois.

The town of Pullman was situated on 3,500 acres that Pullman owned on the shores of Lake Calumet, whose breezes, he was sure, "would produce 10 percent more work." Opposite the factory—whose tall clock tower on the red brick machine works dominated the town—were 1,800 brick homes of "Dutch" design, and an arcade with theater, public library, hotel named after Pullman's 13-year-old daughter Florence, retail shops and stores, a post office, a bank, two churches, and a school. There was a huge recreation field for the town's 9,000 dwellers—three-fourths of whom were immigrants (Scotch, English, Irish, Dutch, Scandinavian, German)—and a park with a bandstand. Except that its ruler's sandstone castle was far to the north on Prairie Avenue, it was an archetypical medieval town, populated by serfs. Except that the serfs' living quarters were far grander, it was a Southern plantation.

No beer gardens or saloons were allowed—though there was a private bar in the Florence Hotel for George M. Pullman's personal guests and visitors. Pullman would fire an employee who dropped a piece of paper in the street and failed to pick it up, and any tenant could be evicted from his home on 10 days' notice for any reason. No labor organizers were permitted within the town's limits; no improper books were permitted in the library or improper plays in the theater. "I shall try and benefit humanity where it is in my power to do so," Pullman avowed. With his model town he was going to show that "such advan-

21

tages and surroundings made better workmen by removing them from the feeling of discontent and desire for change which so generally characterizes the American workman, thus protecting the employer from the loss of time and money consequent upon intemperance, labor strikes and dissatisfaction which generally result from poverty and uncongenial home surroundings."

When the town's theater was formally opened he brought an invited audience of wealthy men and women out from Chicago in six lavish Pullman cars through a heavy snowstorm to hear a lecture on the sanctity of the model town of Pullman. "Everywhere is utility, order, cleanliness, and beauty," noted the speaker. ". . . They must help children, women, and men to grow into sweeter, whiter, nobler, and more productive manhood."

Pullman revenues were scaled to return a 6 percent profit to the Pullman Palace Car Company; rents were 15 percent higher than equivalent housing in Chicago. Residents bought their gas and water from the company, which got it from Chicago, water at four cents per thousand gallons, sold at ten cents to tenants; gas was bought at 33 cents per thousand feet, sold to tenants at $2.25 per thousand feet. The annual fee for use of the public library was $3.00 for adults, $1.00 for children; only 250 families could afford to belong. Even the sewage from the workers' homes was put to profit by George M. Pullman; he had it pumped to his 140-acre farm, where it was spread on the fields as fertilizer. The town's two churches were leased from the company for $300 a month.

On paydays, money owed the Pullman Palace Car Company for rent, gas, water, provisions, and any other bills due was deducted from what the employee had earned. Heads of families, thus, sometimes got only three or four cents in cash on payday. For those families that could not afford the prevailing rents, the town had a special section built specifically for them—a model slum.

In 1893 Chicago held its World's Columbian Exposition to celebrate the 400th anniversary of Columbus' discovery of America. The 686-acre fairgrounds was called the "White City." The winter of the Exposition year in the White City, as the whole of Chicago was by then calling itself, was known as the "Black Winter." One of the nation's recurrent financial panics and depressions had struck and in Chicago people went hungry and died from the cold. Democratic political clubs organized soup kitchens in the winter of '93-'94, and City Hall sheltered 2,000 homeless each night. The 6,000 saloonkeepers of the city fed 60,000 hungry, jobless men a day, even when the men could not afford the nickel beer that was the customary prerequisite of a free lunch.

The Pullman Palace Car Company laid off a third of its work force and wages were cut 30 percent to 40 percent for the rest, though rents remained the same as before. On payday, some workers got nothing and others went into debt to the company. Over the winter workers would faint at their jobs from hunger. Finally, a delegation of 43 workers was sent to discuss these conditions with George M. Pullman.

He refused to meet with them, but fired them all and the next day evicted them from their rented homes.

A group of workers met in a nearby town and there organized a local branch of Eugene Victor Debs' new American Railway Union (ARU). Back in Pullman they recruited more members and demanded restoration of their former wages. When this demand was immediately refused, 3,000 of them went out on strike on May 11th.

George M. Pullman shut down his plant. "I don't know how long the strike will last," he said. "Financially it is a good thing for the stockholders."

When the members of the ARU struck in sympathy with Pullman Palace Car Company workers, it was ruled by the U.S. courts that the courts had the power to issue orders and injunctions in labor disputes affecting the public interest. President Grover Cleveland sent federal troops into Chicago to protect the mails, and following violence and extensive property damage, the courts ordered all strike activities stopped. When Eugene Debs, head of the union, refused, he was held in contempt of court and jailed.

By the end of the first week of the strike, 151 Pullman families were begging for food. The Democratic mayor of Chicago sent thousands of dollars of groceries to the town, paid for out òf his own pocket. The strike chairman at Pullman said, "We do not expect the company to concede our demands. . . . We do know that we are working for less wages than will maintain ourselves and families in the necessaries of life and on that proposition we absolutely refuse to work any longer."

Pullman resolutely declined to submit the dispute to arbitration—arbitration urged on him by many Chicago civic leaders and the mayors of 56 other U.S. cities. The national Republican Party strategist Mark Hanna, hardly known for his pro-labor sentiments, raged that "a man who won't meet his own men halfway is a goddam fool!" Reminded that Pullman had built his workers a model town, Hanna replied, "Model shithouse! Go and live in Pullman and find out how much Pullman gets selling city water and gas . . . to those poor fools!"

The ARU sent Pullman a note pleading with him to meet with the strikers. He refused to open the note. By June 22nd, the ARU had lost its collective patience and delegates to its annual convention (held in Chicago), acting on instructions from their locals, voted unanimously to boycott all Pullman cars beginning on the 26th. "We shall absolutely insist on order," Debs promised.

Though no violence had as yet occurred, U.S. Attorney General Richard Olney—a founder of the General Manager's Association (GMA), a strikebreaking combine of 24 railway lines—obtained a court order July 2nd enjoining the union from interfering with the U.S. mails or interstate commerce. The railroads then attached unnecessary Pullman cars to trains so that ARU members would not handle them—and would thus technically be interfering with the mails and interstate commerce.

On July 2nd, also, over Illinois Governor Altgeld's protests, President Grover Cleveland ordered U.S. troops from Fort Sheridan marched into Chicago. On July 4th the troops pitched their tents around public buildings and along the lake front. Marshall Field, the Pullman Palace Car Company's largest stockholder, publicly expressed his thanks for their presence. When rioting began, railroad cars were overturned and burned—some by gangs of hoodlums hired by the GMA.

By the 9th, the troops had quelled the rioting, but 12 men had been killed and $685,000 worth of property had been destroyed. Without federal intervention, George M. Pullman might have been forced to arbitration.

Debs was indicted on the 10th and, leaderless and starving, the strikers capitulated. When late in August the Pullman plant reopened, new employees had to sign a pledge they would never join a union, and all ARU members rehired were required to surrender their union membership cards.

Many were not rehired—some 1,600—and Governor Altgeld, who had visited the town and found to his horror that 6,000 humans were without food, four-fifths of them women and children, asked Pullman to exhibit some humanity. Pullman refused; he said that to do so would put him in a bad light. Governor Altgeld replied to Pullman, saying of the workers, "I assume that even if they are wrong and had been foolish, you would not be willing to see them perish. . . ."

Pullman—urged on by Marshall Field—declared himself willing, yes, to let them and their families perish; it would be a salutary lesson to the others.

After six months in prison, Eugene V. Debs was released; he came out a confirmed Socialist. Governor Altgeld, who had pardoned the surviving Haymarket prisoners the year before because on investigation he had found that their jury was packed, their judge prejudiced, and that none of the accused had been shown to be guilty, finished out his term as governor knowing his political career was at an end: he had opposed the wishes of the state's business leaders, its power elite.

George M. Pullman died three years after the strike. He left a fortune of $21,000,000. He had spent his life in the pursuit of this wealth, at his own risk and in his own manner, his objective being to maximize profits to the fullest—and the workers be damned. He was buried beneath reinforced concrete and steel, just in case some of his former employees might visit his grave to pay their respects.

Free at Last

When America's War Between the States began in 1861 there were four million black slaves in the South. Seventy years after the Civil War ended some of the still living of those four million (then very old) were interviewed about their lives as slaves. Susan Hamlin, who was a slave in her early thirties during the war, was asked, "Were most of the masters kind?"

"Well, you know," Susan Hamlin responded,

"times den was just like dey is now, some was kind and some was mean; heaps of wickedness went on just de same as now. All my people was good people. I see some wickedness and I hear 'bout all kinds of t'ings but you don't know whether it was lie or not. Mr. Fuller been a Christian man.

". . . I tell you how I t'ink it is. The Lord made t'ree nations, the white, the red and the black, and put dem in different places on de earth where dey was to stay. Dose black ignoramuses in Africa forgot God, and didn't have no religion and God blessed and prospered the white people dat did remember Him and sent dem to teach de black people even if dey have to grab dem and bring dem into bondage till dey learned some sense. The Indians forgot God and dey had to be taught better so dey land was taken away from dem. God sure bless and prosper de white people and He put de red and de black people under dem so dey could teach dem and bring dem into sense wid God. . . ."

These memories and opinions were elicited from a black woman more than 100 years old. Her interviewer was white.

Responding to similar questions, but this time from a black interviewer, Susan Hamlin said:

"W'en any slave was whipped all de other slaves was made to watch. I see women hung frum de ceilin' of buildin's an' whipped with only supin tied 'round her lower part of de body, until w'en dey was taken down, dere wusn't breath in de body. . . ."

To a fellow black, Susan Hamlin apparently felt she could tell more of the truth of what slavery had meant to the enslaved. To her black interviewer, with a quite different emphasis, she gave again her theory of the three races:

"De white race is so brazen. Dey come here an' run de Indians frum dere own lan', but dey couldn't make dem slaves 'cause dey wouldn't stan' for it. Indians use to git up in trees an' shoot dem with poison arrow. W'en dey couldn't make dem slaves den dey gone to Africa an' bring dere black brother an' sister. Dey say 'mong themselves, 'we gwine mix dem up en make ourselves king. Dats de only way we'd get even with de Indians.' "

Were most of the masters kind? Suppose they were; their slaves were still their property and wholly subject to them and their every whim, even as to life and death. Seventy years after she was freed, Susan Hamlin still vividly remembered how it had been:

"All time, night an' day, you could hear men an' women screamin' to de tip of dere voices as either ma, pa, sister, or brother was take without any warnin' an' sell. Some time mother who had only one chile was separated fur life. People wus always dyin' frum a broken heart.
"One night a couple married an' de next mornin' de boss sell de wife. De gal ma got in in de street an' cursed de white woman fur all she could find. She said: 'dat damn white, pale-face bastard sell my daughter who jus' married las' night,' an' other t'ings. The white man tresten' her to call de police if she didn't stop, but de collud woman said: 'hit me or call de police. I redder die dan to stan' dis any longer.' De police took her to de Work House by de white woman orders an' what became of 'er, I never hear. . . ."

One house Negro overheard the news of emancipation while serving dinner to her master and mistress. She excused herself, saying she had to get water from the spring. There, out of sight of the great house she expressed her feelings:

"I jump up and scream, 'Glory, glory hallelujah to Jesus! I'se free! I'se free! Glory to God, you come down an' free us; no big man could do it.' An' I got sort o' scared, afeared somebody hear me, an' I takes another good look, an' fall on de groun' an' roll over, an' kiss de groun' fo' de Lord's sake, I'se so full o' praise to Masser Jesus."

But the exultation lasted only a brief time. All of the North's slaves had been freed by 1820, four decades before the Civil War began (slavery was unprofitable in the North), but anti-black prejudice remained strong there. Many Union soldiers, perhaps the majority, were openly hostile to Southern blacks and even many of the missionaries who came south to the vanquished Confederacy to do good works for the ex-slaves looked upon them with contempt. "I say good-mornin' to my young missus," a black child told a friend, referring to one of the missionaries, "and she say, 'I slap your mouth for your impudence, you nigger.' "

The freedmen and freedwomen discovered they must learn a new kind of circumspection in dealing with whites. . . . Well, not all that new. In most respects it was the same old same old, and they had to stand it longer, and longer, long after Emancipation, long after they became citizens.

Social Problems

A civilization which tends to concentrate wealth and power in the hands of a fortunate few, and to make of others mere human machines, must inevitably evolve anarchy and bring destruction. But a civilization is possible in which the poorest could have all the comforts and conveniences now enjoyed by the rich; in which prisons and almshouses would be needless, and charitable societies unthought of. Such a civilization waits only for the social intelligence that will adapt means to ends. Powers that might give plenty to all are already in our hands. . . .

"Devil catch the hindmost" is the motto of our so-called civilized society today. We learn early to "take care of No. 1," lest No. 1 should suffer; we learn early to grasp from others that we may not want ourselves. The fear of poverty makes us admire great wealth; and so habits of greed are formed, and we behold the pitiable spectacle of men who have already more than they can by any possibility use, toiling, striving, grasping to add to their store up to the very verge of the grave—that grave which, whatever else it may mean, does certainly mean the parting with all earthly possessions however great they be. . . .

. . . In soil and sunshine, in vegetable and animal life, in veins of minerals, and in pulsing forces which we are only beginning to use, are capabilities which we cannot exhaust—materials and powers from which human effort, guided by intelligence, may gratify every material want of every human creature. There is in nature no reason for poverty—not even for the poverty of the crippled or the decrepit. For man is by nature a social animal, and the family affections and the social sympathies would, where chronic poverty did not distort and embrute, amply provide for those who could not provide for themselves.

But if we will not use the intelligence with which we have been gifted to adapt social organization to natural laws; if we allow dogs in the manger to monopolize what they cannot use; if we allow strength and cunning to rob honest labor, we must have chronic poverty, and all the social evils it inevitably brings. Under such conditions there would be poverty in paradise.

"The poor ye have always with you." If ever a scripture has been wrested to the devil's service, this is that scripture. How often have these words been distorted from their obvious meaning to soothe conscience into acquiescence in human misery and degradation—to bolster that blasphemy, the very negation and denial of Christ's teachings, that the All-Wise and Most Merciful, the Infinite Father, had decreed that so many of his creatures must be poor in order that others of his creatures to whom he wills the good things of life should enjoy the pleasure and virtue of doling out alms! "The poor ye have always with you," said Christ; but all his teachings supply the limitation, "until the coming of the Kingdom." In that kingdom of God *on earth*, that kingdom of justice and love for which he taught his followers to strive and pray, there will be no poor. . . . Queer ideas of the Divinity have some of these Christians who hold themselves orthodox and contribute to the conversion of the heathen. A very rich orthodox Christian said to a newspaper reporter, awhile ago, on the completion of a large work out of which he is said to have made millions: "We have been peculiarly favored by Divine Providence; iron never was so cheap before, and labor has been a drug in the market."

That in spite of all our great advances we have yet with us the poor, those who, without fault of their own, cannot get healthful and wholesome conditions of life, is *our* fault and *our* shame. Who that looks about him can fail to see that it is only the injustice that denies natural opportunities to labor, and robs the producer of the fruits of his toil, that prevents us all from being rich? Consider the enormous powers of production now going to waste; consider the great number of unproductive consumers maintained at the expense of producers. . . . Consider how much brains and energy and capital are devoted, not to the production of wealth, but to the grabbing of wealth. Consider the waste caused by competition which does not increase wealth; by laws which restrict production and exchange. Consider how human power is lessened by insufficient food, by unwholesome lodgings, by work done under conditions that produce disease and shorten life. Consider how intemperance and unthrift follow poverty. Consider how the ignorance bred of poverty lessens production, and how the vice bred of poverty causes destruction, and who can doubt that under conditions of social justice all might be rich?

The wealth-producing powers that would be evoked in a social state based on justice, where wealth went to the producers of wealth, and the banishment of poverty had banished the fear and greed and lusts that spring from it, we now can only faintly imagine. . . .

The foregoing words, each and every one, were written by Henry George, an American economist, and were published in 1883 (more than a century ago) in his book *Social Problems*. I certainly endorse the sentiments but obviously the trend's been accelerating in a direction opposite to their author's wishful thinking.

In the spring of 1996 Congressional Democrats were supporting a bill to raise the minimum wage in the United States from $4.25 an hour to $5.15 an hour over a two-year period. Big deal. It was calculated at the time that a minimum wage of $7.00 an hour would be necessary to enable a family of three to live at the poverty level. Ten million Americans worked at the minimum wage. To make ends meet they usually worked at two, sometimes three jobs.

Nevertheless, House Republicans, led by Speaker Newt Gingrich, with a rabid pack of 70 blown-dry-coiffured freshmen Republican representatives behind him, denounced the bill. They very vehemently did not want to raise the minimum wage. They realized that 1996 was an election year and that their stand might hurt them slightly in the polling places but they were men of principle: If you raised the minimum wage, said CEOs of powerful corporations, you might diminish corporate profits. And corporations had paid the congressmen's way into Congress.

House Republicans maintained that their purpose in opposing the minimum-wage raise was to protect the middle class. How? And, even if so, might they not have done more humanly to help, by however so little, the underclass, the "ghetto" class, that worked at the minimum-wage rate? But of course the House Republicans were not beholden to that class. No one in any position of power in America at the end of the 20th century was.

Back in 1883, Henry George also wrote:

Nor should we forget that in civilized man still lurks the savage. The men who, in past times, oppressed or revolted, who fought to the death in petty quarrels and drunk fury with blood, who burned cities and rent empires, were men essentially such as those we daily meet. Social progress has accumulated knowledge, softened manners, refined tastes and extended sympathies, but man is yet capable of as blind a rage as when, clothed in skins, he fought wild beasts with a flint. And present tendencies, in some respects at least, threaten to kindle passions that have so often before flamed in destructive fury.

A Lazy Summer

In the summer of 1952 I spent some time in the South and on its fringes. I had never been there before. In some respects, I was like the country priest who refutes the Manichean without having troubled to inquire what the Manichean believes. (A paraphrase of Ortega y Gasset—yet one more hangover from my liberal arts higher education.)

My first discovery was that Kansas City, Missouri, was a city of cigar smokers and beautiful girls. Small, beautiful girls who wore a rounding-type brassiere that gave their breasts under their summer dresses the appearance of large, soft, round plums. It was also a city of religious bookstores and chiropractors. A young Marlon Brando in *Viva Zapata* was playing to large crowds in a movie house in the Mexican section of the city. Not a soul in that mostly Latino-packed theater actually cried out, "*Viva Zapata!*" however.

The American Legion was holding a Department Convention in a downtown hotel. An "IMPORTANT NOTICE" left in the Legionnaires' rooms warned them against tomfoolery. "We are a great organization," it said, "doing a great and worthwhile job. Yet, a few irresponsible pranksters, on a convention spree, can completely discount, in the eyes of the public, all that we are accomplishing." They all got drunk, anyway, and threw ice water and other materials and objects out of the hotel's windows.

In the cheap, workers' cafes, next to reproductions of Murilloesque Virgins and Christ Childs above the cash registers, was always a sign saying in big, bold caps: "WE RESERVE THE RIGHT TO REFUSE SERVICE TO ANYONE."

In Forrest City, Arkansas, outside the home I stayed in, the locusts had set up their incessant whine and on the lawn below my upstairs window a little girl was calling to her daddy, who was watering the lawn, "Daddy, wet mah fooaht, Daddy, wet my fooaht." The little white boys and girls in this neighborhood are all rather small and peaked, with great big eyes and skinny arms and legs. In the rest of town all the little black kids are cute as hell and smile at you and say, "Hi!"

Very dry this summer. On either side of Crowley's ("Crooley's") Ridge, 5 miles wide, 135 miles long, is what they call the Delta, very flat, sandy soil. The St. Francis River is as low as it's been in 20 years and the cotton is no good this year. They also grow rice and truck produce here. Mostly it's Negroes who do the farming. On shares. In most years the Delta floods; in wet years for two or three months at a time.

The houses of the Negroes stand on pyramidal cement blocks, a foot or so high, in the fields, near the road. The front porch sags, the shutters hang by one hinge, when the windows have shutters, and the siding hasn't been painted since the houses were built. Junk is piled in the front yard to one side and out back around the privy, which is in worse shape than the house.

The front door, if there is one, is always open, and, right inside, the lady of the house is cooking in the front room, which also, on the evidence of two cots that can be seen, serves as a bedroom. In fact, the front room seems to be the only room the house has.

Everyone visits everyone else on Sunday. They sit out in the front yard and chat. In the evening the circle of empty chairs out front tells you it's been Sunday. There's a place below the highway coming into town where there is a cluster of tumbledown houses. One evening on the front porch of one of these houses a good-looking, young, Negro woman is stretched out in a hammock in her Sunday best, watching the cars go by, a glass of something in her hand.

Sitting to her right on two chairs catty-wampus to one another are a younger girl about 15 or 16 who I take to be her kid sister, also in her best and neatest, and in the other chair the girl's boyfriend, wearing a T-shirt and chinos, holding the kid sister's hand and slowly, very slowly, lifting and lowering it between them, all the while looking longingly into the girl's eyes. There is a shy smile on his face. She is looking back at him, her expression grave but friendly. The older sister in the hammock remains intent on watching the cars go by.

Forrest City's population in July of 1952 is 7,600. Somebody in a cafe tells me this is "7,000 niggers and 600 whites." The town has a radio station and its own weekly newspaper.

In Chicago the country's political parties are meeting to nominate their candidates for President. The Democratic Party's platform plank on civil rights endorses federal action to secure equal employment opportunity to everyone, the right to security of all persons, and the right to full and equal participation in the nation's political life. The Republican plank on civil rights leaves these matters to the discretion of the individual states.

34

In Forrest City the Negroes have their own waiting rooms at public places, their own cafes and laundries, their own movie house, and pretty much their own section of town. The "White" drinking fountains are white porcelain—but so are those for "Colored."

In New York, Tommy Manville, heir to an immense asbestos fortune, runs a full-page ad in newspapers stating that "Tommy Manville, Jr., is no longer responsible for any bills incurred by his ninth wife, Anita Eden Manville." The couple has been married for almost two weeks.

You see a white-haired, old, crippled-up Negro who's maybe never in his life lifted up his head to look a white man in the eye, all bent over, holding the small of his back with one hand while with the other he daubs polish on the shoes of the white man who owns the second-hand clothing store that caters to Negroes in Forrest City.

You see a fine-looking young man with his good-looking wife and two young children sitting patiently in the Colored Waiting Room at the bus depot. If the husband is a cook in a white man's cafe, they let him double as garbage remover when the garbage truck pulls up in back. The Luncheon Special is smothered hamburger with your choice of three of the following: stewed potatoes, stewed tomatoes, turnip greens, or pickled cucumber salad. The young white cashier at the cafe hands you your change. She says, "Y'all come back, *hear?*"

The landlady of the house I am staying at is middleaged but not matronly and speaks in the high, little girl's voice that most women affect in Forrest City, with a sugared, "soft" southern accent. She brings a glass of ice water up to my room the first evening. "I'm sorry about the looks," she says, gesturing at the floor, "but the nigger splattered paint all over when he painted."

Her husband tells me they are "just poor country folks, just like everybody else in town." It is a phrase he uses often; three or four times he assures me that he and his wife are "just poor country folks." He has 400 acres in rice and 400 in cotton this year. His farm is 15 miles out of town and he gets up at 6 o'clock every morning to go out to it, talk to his sharecroppers. He asks me if I'd like to go to church with them that evening, "just a little country church."

In Chicago at the Democratic convention Eleanor Roosevelt is introduced to the delegates in the packed amphitheater as "the first lady of the world" and a great torrent of sound floods down to the stage as the delegates and spectators cheer and cheer. Twenty years before, in the depths of the Depression, her husband had stood in the same place and accepted the party's nomination for President and called for a New Deal in national life. Eleanor Roosevelt stands before this generation's delegates a revered figure, recalling a time that is gone but whose spirit may still linger.

Adlai E. Stevenson, the 1952 Democratic nominee for President, is a gradualist on civil rights. His opponent, Republican Dwight D. Eisenhower, is not even that.

The house I stay at in Forrest City is full of small pictures of the saints and the Virgin Mary and the Christ Child. The living room has a couch, a modern relaxation chair, a lamp with a red velvet shade, a complicated chromium lamp with a built-in clock, a fireplace whose mantel is cluttered with bric-a-brac, a TV set, and a small end table on which rests the Holy Bible. The heads of two magnificent buck deer are mounted on one wall.

My landlord has an arrangement with the mayor of Forrest City and the banker-farmer who lives directly across the street (not the banker-farmer who lives on the corner) where in the fall they go south to the 1920 acres of timber they own there (three sections) and have a stand built. (My landlord estimates that 75 percent of the people who live in Forrest City own farms; he speaks of the favored 600.) They rest and drink and wait on the stand until their dogs and "the niggers on horseback" drive deer by it. Then they shoot themselves a deer.

I notice that there are a helluva lot of blind and crippled people in Forrest City. Blacks. I mean to ask why, but I never get around to it. I understand that liberal arts graduates today are still the questioning sort, only they have to get around to asking. The first question out of their mouths after graduation today, I'm told, is, "Will you want fries with that?"

The Manicheans believe that the universe is controlled by two antagonistic powers: (1) Light (spirit, good) and (2) Darkness (matter, evil). I *think* the Manicheans—a lot of them, at any rate—weren't quite certain which power would triumph in the world, good or evil. Perhaps they still don't know. Perhaps the issue is still in doubt.

The glass in which my landlady had brought me ice water is empty. Outside, below the screen on my bedroom window, the little girl implores her daddy to "Help me turn it ooahff, Daddy, help me turn it ooahff!"

> "The big bee flies high,
> The little bee makes the honey;
> The black folks makes the cotton
> And the white folks gets the money."

The Codes

Twain's and Warner's *The Gilded Age* was published in 1873, eight years after the close of the Civil War. While the book has as its chief target congressional corruption and the pillage of the nation's resources that followed the war, it also took sidelong thrusts at other scandals of the times, one of which was the question of what to do with or for or to the freedman—the ex-slave, the Negro.

Here is an exchange between the novel's oleaginous Senator Dilworthy and its speculation-crazed Colonel Beriah Sellars; the Senator is speaking:

> "Providence," he said, "has placed them in our hands, and although you and I, General, might have chosen a different destiny for them, under the Constitution, yet Providence knows best."
>
> "You can't do much with 'em," interrupted Col. Sellers. "They are a speculating race, sir, disinclined to work for white folks without security, planning how to live by only working for themselves. Idle, sir, there's my garden just a ruin of weeds. Nothing practical in 'em."
>
> "There is some truth in your observation, Colonel, but you must educate them."
>
> "You educate the niggro and you make him more speculating than he was before. If he won't stick to any industry except for himself now, what will he do then?"
>
> "But, Colonel, the negro when educated will be more able to make his speculations fruitful."
>
> "Never, sir, never. He would only have a wider scope to injure himself. A niggro has no grasp, sir. Now, a white man can conceive great operations, and carry them out; a niggro can't."
>
> "Still," replied the Senator, "granting that he might injure himself in a worldly point of view, his elevation through

education would multiply his chances for the hereafter—which is the important thing after all, Colonel. And no matter what the result is, we must fulfill our duty by this being."

"I'd elevate his soul," promptly responded the Colonel; "that's just it; you can't make his soul too immortal, but I wouldn't touch *him*, himself. Yes, sir! make his soul immortal, but don't disturb the niggro as he is."

The Senator and the Colonel manage between them to plan a great operation to aid the Negro: They know of a large, barren tract of land in Tennessee (owned by a friend); they apprehend that this scrub land will be an ideal location on which to establish a school for the freedman; the government must buy it for that purpose; the fair price will be $3 million—though the land has failed in many previous attempts to find a buyer, even at $7,000 for the whole.

As the authors note somewhat later in their work, "If you should rear a duck in the heart of the Sahara, no doubt it would swim if you brought it to the Nile."

The Black Codes of the antebellum South, adopted formally in the early 1800s, had prescribed the slave's legal standing. They held that:

1) Negro testimony was inadmissible against whites;
2) Slaves could make no contracts or own property;
3) Slaves could be punished at will;
4) No slave could raise his hand against a white man;
5) The rape of a female slave was not rape—it was trespassing.

After Emancipation the codes remained as the mind-set of Southern whites, and restricted the lives and shadowed the thoughts of many, many blacks, particularly as the Codes were reinstated and expanded by the individual southern states.

No very great intelligence was applied to the social problems faced by the South after the Civil War. The South had no plan for reconstruction and the North was divided between leniency and retribution. The policy toward the conquered of Lincoln's successor, the Tennessean Andrew Johnson, though scarcely benign, was not harsh enough to satisfy the Radical Republicans of Congress, who wanted to punish the South for its secession. In 1866, after nearly two years of wrangling with Congress, Johnson came within one vote of impeachment.

The civil rights act passed by Congress that same year (over Johnson's veto, the first time Congress ever overrode a presidential veto), was superseded by the 14th Amendment, ratified in 1868, which guaranteed citizenship to Negroes and equality under the law. Another civil rights act passed by Congress in 1875 prohibited discrimination against Negroes in public establishments and railroads and other carriers. This act was overturned in 1883 on the grounds that these were social, not civil rights.

Immediately after the war the state governments of the South came under the control of blacks, northern carpetbaggers and scalawags (southerners who worked with the blacks and carpetbaggers) who set out to humiliate the plantation owners and enrich themselves, and by 1870 anarchy and crime were widespread in the South. Its old rulers, the planters, had been systematically degraded by federal and state actions, but gradually the planter aristocracy began to reassert control. By the end of the 1870s white supremacy was once again in the ascendant in the South, blacks were effectively denied citizenship, and the South was solidly Democratic in its politics, as it was to remain for the next 70 years.

In 1890 Louisiana passed a law "requiring all railway companies carrying passengers on their trains in this state, to provide equal but separate accommodations for the white and colored races." Two years later, Homer Plessy, seven-eighths white and one-eighth Negro, claimed in a New Orleans court that the law was racially segregationist, and therefore unconstitutional under the 13th and 14th Amendments. The judge ruled against Plessy.

The case went to the Supreme Court, which in 1896 in *Plessy v. Ferguson* ruled that blacks who felt demeaned by segregation were suffering from an inferiority complex, nothing more. The Court said that "legislation is powerless to eradicate racial instincts" and made into law the doctrine of "separate but equal." (Justice John Marshall Harlan wrote a dissent. He argued that, in "the view of the Constitution, in the eye of the law, there is in this country no superior, dominant ruling class of citizens. There is no caste here. Our Constitution is colorblind, and neither knows nor tolerates classes among citizens.")

To reconstruct the South as a whole, healthy, cohesive region harboring two races would have required that its Negroes be given the vote and full civil liberties; that they be educated; that whites abandon discrimination; and, perhaps most important it would have required the implementation of some kind of land reform.

At the end of the Civil War many ex-slaves believed that the government would give each black family 40 acres and a mule by way of some small recompense for generations of unpaid labor. Initially the government strongly encouraged this belief. "Gib us our own land and we take care ourselves," one freedman observed, "but widout land, de ole massas can hire us or starve us, as dey please." In the event, no freedman got so much as a swaybacked mule, never mind 40 acres.

No land, no real freedom. Had Negroes been able to buy land and earn from it they might possibly have accumulated enough economic power to seize the vote for themselves and build adequate schools for their children. But state laws were passed forbidding them to own land.

Even had they been permitted to own land, Negroes could not have bought it; they were destitute at Emancipation and, in any case, did not earn enough from their daily labor to afford even the poorest southern acreage. They still supplied most of the field labor, household help, and skilled workmen in the South, but they lived in virtual peonage. They could not vote; they could not mingle with whites in schools, public conveyances or places of amusement; they could rarely obtain justice in southern courts; and when white feelings ran high against them they were often lynched—that is hanged by the neck, burned at the stake, murdered and mutilated by a mob.

The Black Codes reinstated after the war had these provisions, among others:

1) Negroes could not own land or houses except in incorporated cities or towns;

2) Negroes could not intermarry or cohabit with whites;

3) Negroes must show a license from police to prove employment;

4) Negroes could be arrested for quitting a job;

5) Negroes could not carry or keep weapons or ammunition;

6) Negroes could not testify in court.

Mississippi's Black Codes also provided that "mischief," "insulting gestures," and the "vending of spiritous or intoxicating liquors" were criminal acts. Mississippi's Vagrancy Act provided that ex-slaves found "with no lawful employment" were to be deemed vagrants and fined. Its Enticement Act made it illegal to lure a Negro from his employer by offering inducements.

These measures, gradually put in place throughout the South, assured a large, cheap, tractable supply of labor. They also greatly increased the criminalization of the black population. To manage its growing black prison population, Mississippi in 1876 passed the Leasing Act, which allowed private individuals to rent convicts from state, county, and local prisons. Many of the convicts rented for such labor were children as young as six or seven. The convict-labor lease system spread throughout the South, enabling planters and industrialists to reap considerable fortunes from it. The system lasted into the 1920s, with Alabama being the last state to relinquish it.

By the end of the century the South's ante-bellum race caste system was fully restored. Blacks were no longer slaves but in very many ways they were worse off than if they had been. The quest for equal rights for blacks had hit bottom; it stayed there for another quarter century.

In 1828, Thomas D. Rice, a popular, white entertainer who performed in black face, inspired by a Negro stage driver's singing (or a young black boy in an alley, or an old stablehand named Jim

Crow—accounts vary), had introduced this ditty into a Pittsburgh performance of his minstrel show (minstrelsy became a national craze):

> "Wheel about, turn about,
> Do just so.
> Every time I wheel about,
> I jump Jim Crow."

As the 19th century ended, Jim Crow was once again the race relations policy of the white South—and not noticeably absent in the North. There were nine million blacks in the country, seven million of these in the South, and their one best hope, it seemed, would remain the glories of the hereafter. There they would still be black—but no one would notice. (As a matter of fact, many ex-slaves didn't believe whites would go to heaven.)

Samuel Insull (1859-1938)
(Chicago Historical Society)

Italian-American family, Chicago, ca. 1915.
(University of Illinois at Chicago, The University Library, Jane Addams
Collection)

Ozymandias

Samuel Insull, Jr., was born in London in 1859, the son of a Congregationalist preacher and temperance crusader. At 14 he left school to become an office boy. He taught himself shorthand and accounting, but at 19 was discharged from his job because his employer found a doting father who was willing to *pay* for the privilege of having his son keep the accounts that Samuel Insull, Jr., had been keeping for over four years for a weekly wage of five shillings ($1.25). "My experience is that the greatest aid in the efficiency of labor is a long line of men waiting at the gate," Insull was to observe many years later.

He found his next employment as the secretary of Thomas Edison's English agent and in 1881—at the age of 21—came to the United States as Edison's personal secretary. He was soon managing the 33-year-old Edison's business affairs; he held Edison's power of attorney, signed his checks, worked day and night. But in 1892, when the eastern Edison companies were merged by the elder J. P. Morgan to create General Electric, he accepted the presidency of Chicago Edison, one of Chicago's 40 power companies, and came west. The directors of Chicago Edison had asked him to recommend the best available man for the job; he determined that that man was himself.

(To purchase stock in the company as a bona fide of his good intent and to establish stature in the LaSalle Street financial community, he was forced to borrow $250,000 from Marshall Field.)

In Chicago he continued to work day and night, pioneering in the use of ever-larger transmission coverage. By 1907 he had formed Commonwealth Edison out of Chicago's many electricity suppliers; by 1911, Public Service Company of Northern Illinois out of another 80 firms. "Very early I discovered," he said, "that the first essential, as in other public utility business, was that it should be operated as a monopoly."

In 1912 Insull created Middle West Utilities, a holding company.

Its capitalization was typical of his financing methods. Twelve million dollars' worth of common and preferred was issued, roughly half of which was "water," that is, stock unsecured by assets. As his self-conferred reward, he received, gratis, $5 million worth of stock—or more, depending upon how the complicated transaction was entered on the books. (It will be recalled that Insull was a self-taught accountant.)

By 1917 Middle West was operating in 11 states, and within another decade Insull's companies were supplying power in 32 of the 48 states of the Union and Canada. He also owned Commonwealth Edison's best customer, Chicago Elevated Railways, as well as Chicago's three electric railroads (he was now a traction as well as a utility magnate), and People's Gas, Light, and Coke Company.

The Insulls lived in a Gold Coast apartment at 1100 Lake Shore Drive, had a 30-room Italian villa country estate, Hawthorn Farm (4,300 acres), near Libertyville in the Skokie Valley north of Chicago, a home in England, and Samuel Insull had a private aerie ("Insull's Throne") all his own atop the $20 million Chicago Civic Opera House, an Insull-built 42-story office building with a huge, ground-level auditorium on the Chicago River. Foreign governments decorated him, American universities awarded him honorary degrees, newspaper editorialists applauded his endeavors.

Toward his employees he practiced a paternalistic benevolence—and fired them if they neglected to greet him with "Good morning, Mr. Insull." He dictated terms to politicians, labor leaders, and bankers, buying their obedience or coercing it.

His public relations staff, headed by the publicist who at his instructions during World War I had spurred on U.S. intervention in England's behalf, projected an image of Insull corporate beneficence—the lowest rates to consumers, the highest returns to investors—which the public embraced wholeheartedly. By the end of the Twenties, a million people owned shares in Insull companies, the vast majority of them small investors, many of them Insull employees and customers and their neighbors and friends in Chicago and the Midwest. ("You are always thinking of the money angle," Thomas Edison had told his young secretary.)

By 1929 Insull was on the board of 85 corporations, the chairman of 65, the president of 11. He controlled a $4-billion empire. In 1929 he founded Insull Utility Investments out of two holding companies purchased in the East—where he came face to face with Morgan interests. (The $10 million of his own securities that he exchanged for Insull Utility Investments quickly soared to a market value of $143 million.)

It has been estimated that shortly before the stock market crash in 1929, Insull company securities were increasing in value at a round-the-clock rate of $7,000 a minute. In just 50 days before the Crash, they appreciated more than half a billion dollars, and Insull's own wealth rose to a reported $170 million. But within three years he and his companies were mired deep in the Great Depression.

The precipitous descent in Insull's fortunes began in 1931 when he bought out Cleveland financier Cyrus Eaton's interest in Insull properties to forestall Eaton's sale of them to Wall Street. This cost Insull $56 million, $40 million of which he had to borrow, half of this from New York bankers.

And then the market in Insull securities broke, helped to its quick and disastrous conclusion by House of Morgan manipulators on the Exchange and rumors of Insull's incapacity (he was 72 and, as always, overworking). By the middle of December of 1931, to keep his superpower ship afloat, Insull had pledged as collateral all of the securities he owned or controlled.

Early in April of 1932 he went to New York to discuss ways of refinancing a routine $10 million Middle West Utilities note due in June. After two afternoons of conferences, Owen D. Young, the chairman of General Electric, broke the news to him: New York bankers would put up no more money. "Does this mean a receivership?" Insull asked.

It did, and Insull was at that instant "too broke to go bankrupt," as one New York banker phrased it. His fall took with him, of course, the million or so investors who had placed their faith—and savings—in his omnipotence. Chicagoans alone lost at least $2 billion. Bank after bank failed in the city because of Insull's ruin.

It required an entire day of dictating and signatures to resign all of his corporate offices, and then he fled to Canada. Then to Paris, then Italy, and finally to Greece, which had no extradition treaty with the United States—an important consideration, since a Cook County grand jury had been asked to indict him for embezzlement and larceny.

He stayed in Greece 19 months before being driven out to Turkey, where he was arrested and returned to the United States. There, he spent a night in the Cook County Jail when his attorney was unable to immediately raise his bail. Some Chicagoans professed to feel sorry for him because he was being treated "as if he were a common criminal."

In October of 1934 he went on trial on a federal indictment for use of the mails to defraud the small investors who at his urging had entrusted their savings to his management. It had been discovered that, under the Insull system of keeping accounts, expenses were entered on his companies' books as assets—which meant that half the income reported year after year by a company such as Middle West Utilities, for example, was fictitious, that it had all been an exercise in smoke and mirrors. Insull took the stand, recounted his humble London beginnings, wept, admitted that he might—yes, he might—have made a $10 million error in his accounts, but swore it was an honest mistake.

The jury voted acquittal.

In the spring of 1935 he was acquitted of the charge of embezzlement, and three months later the trial judge on the last of Insull's federal indictments instructed the jury to bring in a verdict of not guilty. Money never goes to jail.

Three years later, at the age of 79, Insull was felled by a heart attack in a Paris subway. His pockets held only a handkerchief monogrammed "SI" and seven francs, seven centimes (85¢). He left his heirs $10,000 in cash and $14 million in debts.

Barriers

During the earliest years of Reconstruction, large numbers of Negroes had voted in the South. In 1879 Senator William Windom of Minnesota, speaking about southern views on race, stated that "the black does not excite antagonism because he is black, but because he is a *citizen*, and as such may control an election."

Speaking directly for the South about a year earlier, the editor of the Lexington, Missouri, *Tribune* had put Windom's opinion almost as forthrightly: "No simian-souled, sooty-skinned, kink-curled, blubber-lipped, prehensile-heeled, Ethiopian gorilla shall pollute the ballot box with his leprous vote."

The 14th Amendment to the U.S. Constitution, ratified in 1868, made ex-slaves citizens "of the United States and of the State wherein they reside." In its second section it stipulated that if the right of citizens to vote "is denied to any of the male inhabitants of such State, being twenty-one years of age, and citizens . . ., the basis of representation therein shall be reduced in the proportion which the number of such male citizens shall bear to the whole number of male citizens twenty-one years of age in such State."

Despite this seemingly emphatic deterrent, when the planter aristocracy felt its control was strong enough, first Mississippi, South Carolina, and Louisiana (all states in which blacks outnumbered whites), and then other southern states amended their state constitutions in order to disenfranchise Negroes. The "Grandfather Clause," for example, exempted all persons who were voters or descendants of voters on January 1, 1867, from all other basic qualifications for voting. Since one of the basic qualifications was literacy, the Grandfather Clause permitted most poor whites to vote, but at the same time prevented most blacks from voting. Mississippi's test for literacy was typical; it required the prospective voter to read aloud a section of the state constitution, understand it while reading it, and give an interpretation of it. Pass or fail was determined by white registrars.

The Pittsburgh *Dispatch* editorialized over Mississippi's efforts to avoid giving the Negro the vote:

> They are making a fearful and wonderful constitution down in Mississippi. Things from the heavens above and the earth beneath and the waters under the earth are being dragged into the constitution as qualifications for the franchise. In the endeavor to fence the negroes out from political power the Mississippians have concocted some of the queerest legal dishes ever seen. . . . They have not yet decided to disfranchise the man who wears number twelve boots, or the unfortunate who has corns, or the villain who plays the banjo, or the enthusiast who loves "watermillions." But they would travel to their destination by a short cut if they disfranchised every man whose face is not white.

Another southern device for disenfranchising the Negro was the poll tax. By making payment of such a tax one of the basic qualifications to the exercise of the right to vote, the South's planter class not only disenfranchised almost all Negroes, but did the same to many poor whites. This was not a wholly unintended consequence. The Southern aristocracy had possibly as much contempt for poor whites as for blacks, since poor whites were a standing dissent to the claim that any white man was superior to every Negro. The poll tax was not a large sum—$2.00 in Mississippi (though it is true that an ex-slave's cash income was minuscule)—but in some states it was made cumulative—with penalties—from election to election.

While the language of the second section of the 14th Amendment would seem to have outlawed such denials of equal suffrage as the South devised, justice is served not if the laws are in place, but whether or not they are enforced. It was not until 1915 that the Supreme Court declared any of the various southern efforts to disenfranchise the Negro unconstitutional (they acted on the Grandfather Clause). Had Section 2 of the 14th Amendment been enforced, southern representation in the House might have been reduced by as much as 40 percent.

Because of the restrictions imposed formally—and informally (fraud, intimidation, murder)—on Negro voters in the South, only one out of four qualified voters there cast ballots on election day. In the North, three out of four did. The post-Civil War South was solidly Democratic, and since Southern states tended to perpetuate their congressmen, and because chairmen of standing committees in Congress gained that elevation by seniority, when the Democrats controlled Congress the nation's congressional leaders came from a region in which only 25 percent of the electorate voted, at best. At least half of those who did not vote were given no choice; they were not permitted to vote.

This would not seem to be a healthy situation if governments do, indeed, derive their just powers from the consent of the governed. In 1776 the rule of King George III of England over the American colonies was disputed because the king refused to pass laws for large districts of people unless those people would relinquish the right of representation, "a Right inestimable to Them, and formidable to Tyrants only." But for a century in the United States after the Civil War the denial of the right to representation to the southern Negro citizen was treated as a light and transient cause.

In the Old South, Negroes were considered incapable of learning. Together with an assumption of moral inferiority to the white went an assumption of intellectual inferiority, as well. Before the Civil War, only household slaves received even a rudimentary education.

In the eyes of many ex-slaves no prize was so coveted as instruction in reading, writing, and arithmetic, not even land. In the first years after Emancipation, the Freedman's Bureau sent northern teachers to the South; classes were held in make-do schoolrooms or ramshackle Negro churches, often at night, but even so were full and enthusiastic. In Georgia at that time an ex-slave said to his teacher, "We work all day, but we'll come to you in the evening for learning, and we want you to make us learn; we're dull but we want you to beat it into us." In Virginia a school official remarked that ex-slaves were "*crazy* to learn."

In the North, blacks went to public schools only with other blacks, because of residential separation. These de facto segregated schools (just as northern churches were segregated) were inferior to northern white schools. In the South, the schools established in early Reconstruction times for blacks were also inferior to white schools, but when the resurgent planter class regained control of local governments they dispersed even these.

The public schools then established by the planter class for Negroes were also inferior to southern schools for white children, vastly inferior, and classes were held in them usually only four months of the year; the other eight months the pupils' labor was needed in the fields. Even so, the planter class protested that schools for white children were not as good as they might be because available funding had to be shared with the separate Negro school system.

There was truth in this claim; it would have been financially impossible for southern school districts to maintain separate but equal facilities for whites and blacks. But the ruling class in the South had no interest in educating ex-slaves equally. To do so would have disrupted the race caste order. Educated Negroes would discover good reason for dissatisfaction with the status quo. Even when vocational and agricultural schools were established in the South to enable Negroes to train as domestic servants and menial laborers, the training was done with outmoded and discarded techniques and equipment. White Southerners felt that if they expended a good-faith effort to educate blacks, it might encourage them to be uppity, perhaps leave the plantation. And that would have been disastrous, for as one Mississippi planter admitted after the war: "I never did a day's work in my life, and don't know how to begin."

Economically, the southern Negro was essential as cheap labor; the Negro must do those jobs that no self-respecting white man would. It was lack of education that qualified Negroes for these weak-mind, strong-back tasks. The story teller Joel Chandler Harris had his Uncle Remus put it this way as to education: "Hit's de ruinashun er dis country. . . . Put a spelling-book in a nigger's han's, en right den en dar you loozes a plow-hand."

Thus it had been, thus it would ever be. Otherwise, what was privilege for?

So thought and acted the South. In the North, where Negroes were not so omnipresent, the attitude toward them may have been best expressed in this exchange from Mark Twain's *Huckleberry Finn* between Aunt Sally and Huck after a steamboat blows out a cylinder head:

"Good gracious! anybody hurt?"

"No'm. Killed a nigger."

"Well, it's lucky because sometimes people do get hurt."

Whistling Dixie

In June of 1956 I found myself in Chicago, living close by to Lake Michigan. A city employee who worked in Lincoln Park told me a story. I have transcribed it faithfully below, but to this day I don't know whether or not to believe it happened.

I was stabbing paper in the park with my trusted paper-stabber, a rusty nail tied to the end of a cast-off cane, when this finely dressed, elderly gentleman came up to me and spoke.

"As a private citizen," he said, "can I be sued for the denial of civil rights to Negroes?"

"No," I instantly replied, "of course not. As a private citizen you are not legally responsible for anything you merely allow to happen."

"Oh," he sighed. "What a relief to know that."

"However," I went on, "you are allowed to feel morally responsible. That's entirely permissible under the law."

"Quite all right," he said, "I don't and won't. I am from the South. I am a Southern gentleman."

"It was my thought that you had a noble air about you, sir," I responded. "May I ask where you are from in the South?"

"Mississippi." He said it with bravura.

"By 'denial of civil rights to Negroes,' then, you refer to the fact that your great and good native state, with a population of 2,178,914 has only 8 percent registered voters?"

"I do."

"And has eight representatives in Congress. Or one for every 21,800 registered voters. While Montana, for instance and on the other hand, with a population of 591,024—but very few Negroes—has 65 percent registered voters voting for only four representatives, or one for every 86,290 registered voters. In other words, representation in Congress

51

for the two states is far from equal. Your home state of Mississippi, with half the number of registered voters that Montana has, has twice as many representatives. Four times Montana's representation."

"Indeed it does. Good cause, I feel, for Montana's sheepishness."

"In Mississippi you prevent most Negroes—and even some whites—from voting, do you not? By the poll tax if possible, by other means, even force, when necessary?"

"We Southern gentlemen do, certainly,"

"As I thought. You are quite within your rights, sir. You cannot be sued for denying Negroes the right to vote. . . . With public officials, however, the case is altered. They are held responsible for what they permit to happen when they have a positive and legal duty to prevent it."

"To whom, sir," he said, "do you refer?"

"To the President of the United States, of course. Dwight David Eisenhower. As we are both aware, he has sworn to uphold the Constitution."

"And. . .?"

"And Section 2 of the 14th Amendment to the Constitution declares that when the right to vote at any state or federal election is denied or in any way abridged by a state, the basis of representation of that state shall be reduced proportionate to the denial."

"But galloping thoroughbreds, my good man! that would strip we Mississippians of three-fourths of our Congressional representatives! Nay, more! It would strip the entire South of almost half its representation!"

"Steady, sir, steady. You Southern Democrats need not be alarmed. Section 2 has never been enforced. And will not be."

"But what of Attorney General Brownell's call for action on civil rights? Perhaps he will alert the President to this time bomb in the Constitution. Is it not his duty so to do?"

"Never. The President is not to be disturbed, sir. He has vowed to perfect his golf game. Attorney General Brownell's call is a call for votes, full of sound and fury, signifying November coming up."

"Thank you, thank you. You have set my mind at rest.—You, also, I gather, are a gentleman to the manor born. A Northern gentleman."

"No. Unfortunately I do not have that honor, sir. I am only a simple paper stabber for the great metropolis of Chicago."

"But that cane—I thought—"

"The tool of my profession," I replied, lifting my cane in humble salute. "You, sir, may I say, seem to me a true gentleman—no matter your geographical orientation. That is, by that fine old definition of a gentleman, one who never knowingly causes hurt to any fellow being."

"I think I may say that I am," he responded. "Indeed, in all this world, I hate only two things."

"And they are. . .?"

"Bigots," he replied, "and niggers."

Henry Ford (1863-1947)
(Dictionary of American Portraits)

American landscape. (Photo by Bob Fox)

Heartland Hero

In 1902, during a long strike of Pennsylvania anthracite coal miners for a living wage and safer working conditions, a worker wrote to George F. Baer, president of the Philadelphia and Reading Company and thus an executive with influence in the dispute, appealing for help to end the strike. Baer's reply was: "I beg you not to be discouraged. The rights and interests of the laboring man will be protected and cared for, not by the labor agitators but by the Christian men to whom God in His infinite wisdom has given the control of the property interests of the country and upon the successful management of which so much depends."

. . . Just like they say: To have hope is good; it's the waiting that spoils it.

In 1915, with Europe one year into World War I, here in the United States the lawyer for the people in unpopular causes, Clarence Darrow, testified before a Commission on Industrial Relations (chaired by John D. Rockefeller, Jr.). Darrow volunteered that recently enacted laws purportedly for the benefit of U.S. labor "aren't worth a pinch of snuff."

Asked if the ballot could not sooner achieve the purposes of labor than the use of force, Darrow replied, "If every coal miner in the country should refuse to dig a pound of coal until the mines become the property of the government, they would gain their point in a very short time and a thousand years ahead of the ballot."

Not surprisingly, almost 80 years after Darrow's testimony, workers still felt they were being taken advantage of. For example, working man Edsel B. Ford II, a great-grandson of the founder of the Ford Motor Company, was not making the career progress that he felt he should be. He resented this. He was heard to mutter of his employer that "my family owns the place and I'm not even a vice president." The Ford Motor Company was then, in 1993, a $100 billion enterprise.

Edsel B. Ford II's great-grandfather, Henry Ford, was born in 1863, in the middle years of the Civil War, in America's horse and buggy days. An anti-Semite of the first order, a man who thought "History is more or less bunk," a bullying, short-sighted, reactionary know-nothing, blind in most of his views on most matters—including not only his own best interests but also many of those of the industry he did so much to establish—Henry Ford became in his lifetime a hero to the auto-driving public and an American industrialist icon.

In 1879 at the age of 16 Henry had left the family farm, which he detested, for nine-miles-distant Detroit and taken a job there as a machinist's helper. From 1887 to 1889 he worked for the Detroit Edison Company, starting as night fireman and advancing to chief engineer. (When Thomas Edison died in 1931 one of Henry's most treasured possessions became an apparently empty glass vial labeled "Edison's Last Breath.")

Henry did not smoke, drink, gamble, or play around. Though he could read a blueprint only with great difficulty, he had a mechanical turn and was an inveterate tinkerer and from 1889 until it failed in 1902 he was general superintendent of the Detroit Automobile Company. He built his first successful automobile, the "gasoline buggy," in 1893. In 1903, with partners, he formed the Ford Motor Company, paying a dozen men $1.50 a day to turn out gas buggies. Harold Wills designed the early cars; Joseph Galamba, the four-cylinder Model T, which debuted in 1903 with a top speed of 20 mph.

Before it was discontinued in 1928 to make way for the Model A, the Model T (America's beloved "Tin Lizzie") had attained a top speed of 45 mph and more than 15 million had been sold. Right from the beginning Henry Ford's objective was to manufacture a light, durable, easy-to-maintain, and affordable car. No very great psychic powers are needed to predict how he would have reacted—had he been alive—to his company's 1957 Edsel (a model named after his son, whom he harassed into a too-early grave). The Edsel went out of production two years, two months, and 15 days after its introduction to the buying public, $350 million short of turning a nickel's profit.

Henry's great-grandson, Edsel II, who as we have seen coveted a vice presidency (perhaps as a stepping stone to even greater things, who knows?), was a mediocre student at Babson Institute, a lackluster college in Massachusetts. He had had difficulty in graduating from prep school, and took five years to get a degree from Babson.

His great-grandfather was the kind of employer you would wish on your own worst enemy. The Ford Motor Company was a money manufacturing machine whose secret of extracting huge profits was that it relentlessly drove the men who put the cars together. Fifteen minutes for lunch, three minutes to go to the toilet, speedup all along the line.

The Ford plant was a gigantic sweatshop, a house of fear, with its clocked efficiency enforced by supervisors through threats of layoff or dismissal. Talking was prohibited in the plant, as was smoking. (Harry Bennett, Ford's chief enforcer for many years, once shot a cigar out of a unon official's mouth after warning him smoking was not permitted.) The turnover at Ford each year was four men hired, then quitting or fired, to keep one job filled.

Harry Bennett was a brawling thug and, after Edison, the greatest man Henry Ford said he'd ever met. Bennett's "security force" consisted of several thousand goons, company dicks, watchmen, private detectives, jailbirds, stool pigeons, ex-cons, and syndicate gangsters. When pickets marched around the Rouge plant in 1939 shouting "Solidarity!" they had to make sure they kept out of range of the machine guns Bennett had installed on the roof of the plant. Four of them didn't, and died.

Edsel II started full-time work for the Ford Motor Company in 1974. In the early '80s, to gain "hands-on" experience, he had sales, marketing, and advertising jobs at the Ford and the Lincoln-Mercury divisions, and then other responsibilities at corporate headquarters.

When he was put in charge of the company's credit subsidiary, he told some co-workers, "I must admit I was surprised they offered me this job, because I don't have a solid finance background." He meant he had done poorly in his college accounting courses.

Back in the '60s, while Edsel II was still in prep school, I used to know a black gentlemen name of George who played a Gershwin and Porter piano at the Famous Door in Detroit. George also worked a full shift at Ford during the day. He wasn't all that talkative but sometimes on his breaks he'd open up a little. "Monotonous," was what he said about his day job. George was a veteran of 25 years at Ford, and the Door. He had six kids. "And the supervisors," he said, "they're something else. One dog ass thing after another."

You might say the Famous Door was a singles bar. It had a very long bar that doubled back on itself in a U, with a few tables and the piano in a small area at the back. If you were lonely in Detroit you could meet women there, every one for hire.

One night George was elaborating on the monotony of life on the line. "You want to vary things, you could take a pair of pliers, say, and pop off just one little cog on the end of the window crank. Then one day the owner finds his window don't work no more. See? Or drop a BB in the carburetor. No way to see it. Mostly the engine'll cut out when the owner's going downhill. Only way to fix it is to replace the carburetor."

He looked at me over the rim of his drink. "If my supervisor was giving me a hard time," he said, continuing to hypothesize, "I could let a few go by without doing my job, sure. I might even have had that notion. But if I'd done that, then my supervisor would get his own ass

57

chewed out, wouldn't he, for sending incompletes down the line. You tell me," he said softly, "do I look like someone'd do that to his own supervisor?"

It was so dark in there at the back of the Door I couldn't tell. But you never know: Detroit's a pretty depraved town.

When sales of the Model T took off, Henry Ford ditched his partners and Ford Motor Company became a family-owned business. (Henry's younger brothers hated him.) It stayed that way until 1956 when the family took it public. When the family did that it created "super-voting" shares, Class B common, for itself. These shares hold 40 percent of the voting power in the company. If a family member wants to sell any of his Class B common, a family trust buys it up, ensuring that control stays within the family. Henry's great-grandchildren hold about 35.4 million shares of Class B.

Edsel Ford II doesn't like insinuations that family members have had an easy road to promotion in the company. "I think we carry our load," he said, "and we are Fords 24 hours a day. The rest of the officers of Ford Motor Company shut off being officers when they go home."

Well, some of the workers didn't even *go* home. At least one of them used to play piano at the Famous Door in order to earn enough to support his family.

Edsel also chafes under the burden of serving on boards and raising money for charity just because he carries the Ford name. He said it means he must listen to constant pleas of "Won't you do this for us?" and "Won't you do that for us?" Naturally this irritates him, these incessant calls on his better nature.

For argument's sake, let's say that Edsel II is not a billionaire with his Class B holdings; say he's only half a billionaire. And say he's able to support himself and his family on his salary and the perks and stock options he gets as an official at Ford. If he had his Common B in cash, he could put it out at even a modest 6 percent and be pulling in $30 million a year. Keep compounding that and see what you come up with. Makes his great-grandfather's money machine look like a Pez dispenser. And no matter how shaky Edsel's background is in finance, I doubt that his Class B earnings and appreciation come to less than he could earn on the stock if it were in cash.

We know what happened to most of those 15,000,000 Model T's and the millions of Model A's that followed them and to the millions and millions of sweated man hours that went into their assembly. They lie rusting away in vast yards of junk on the outskirts of towns large and small across the continent. Where is it now, Henry, the glory and the dream, eh?

We are repeatedly instructed that it is the wealthy investors of our country who keep our economy going by supplying jobs to millions of people. If that is the fact of the matter, I should have told Gorge the piano player to turn off his alarm clock, call his supervisor, and ask that his check be mailed to his home.

I appropriated this line of reasoning—with which I concur—from a letter written to *Solidarity* (Jan.-Feb. 1996 issue) by Tim Mills, a United Auto Workers member (Local 592) in Garden Prairie, Illinois. Mills wrote that:

> . . . Jobs are not "supplied" by the rich. We supply the labor to generate all wealth, but we are the last to benefit from the take-off and the first to suffer from the crash.
>
> . . . Ours is the richest nation on earth and yet we can no longer afford a system that puts profits before people and perpetuates gluttonous wealth in the midst of deprivation.
>
> . . . With the current system, a carpenter who spends a lifetime building for the boss may wind up homeless and hungry. The solution is not to trade places with the boss. It's to make room for everyone in the mansion. Can we do this without blowing the whistle on him? I don't think so.

Edsel Ford's cousin, William Clay Ford, also a great-grandchild of Henry and an official at Ford, was in his mid-thirties in 1993 when Edsel spoke out about his stymied career. Bill was a bit more optimistically philosophical about Ford and his career. "When people joined this company, they knew we held this unique position," he said, alluding to the voting power of his family's stock. "So if it makes other people uncomfortable, I guess I'm sorry. But it's a fact of life they're going to have to live with."

Bill was right. He *is* right. Them as has, gets. The story has a happy ending, though. There may yet be a Ford in Ford's future. Both Bill and Edsel are today vice presidents of Ford Motor Company, chewing on bones they never made. Maybe their great-grandfather was right when he said, "The world has been, is, and will be run by mediocre men."

A Dry Season

Cotton is supposed to blossom from the bottom of the stem up, but it's been so dry this summer that the crop is only about a foot high yet, and all blossomed out at the top already and not at the bottoms. It looks spindly enough for a good sneeze to blow away half an acre.

In Columbus, Georgia, last week a soldier from Ft. Benning who had been arrested on a disorderly conduct charge hanged himself by his shirt while his cellmate looked on without attempting to intervene. In New York City, two Negroes fought a knife duel to the death while a small crowd watched.

Outside of Forrest City in the ricefields on the Delta the newest wrinkle is to collect water from a well in a basin at the highest point in the field; then, as it's needed, the water's let out into the contours. Two thousand gallons a minute from the well is usually sufficient to water 200 acres of rice.

They say that share-cropping works as great a hardship on poor whites as it does on Negroes but there are about 50 Negro sharecropper families to every poor white that I've seen. I guess everybody involved realizes who has the bookkeeping advantage, the landlord or the family on shares, but what you gonna do?

At the Forrest City grill, over their 60¢ Special slot on the menu is printed: "It's always a rainy day for the shiftless." . . . If you're not shiftless, are you shifty?

The crew is skipping around now, cable-splicing on the Memphis to Little Rock, not dog-legging as per usual, in order to catch this area while it's dry. They call putting the cable into conduits here "ramming the duck." B. J. "Dynamite" Hall is the senior lineman. He says Fletcher—who had the crew for two years before he did—ruined them; had no experience with cable and didn't care if they went by Bell Standard Practices or not. This morning Hall almost fired Prindle for saying he'd use muslin instead of rag to rest the sleeve on. Something like that. Hall

61

also chewed out the whole crew about sawing cable, letting filings get into the coax.

There's another reason we're skipping around: the big-wigs in Kansas City at Long Lines can't make up their minds. This makes B. J. Hall angry. He says all Kansas City cares about is keeping the plow train moving. Sometimes the cable is short (it slipped), necessitating two splices. Sometimes it's too long, has to be cut. But keep the train moving, Hall says, that's all they know in Kansas City. They don't care how you leave it behind—fences hanging, roads tore up—as long as the train keeps moving.

The big shots in Kansas City have a lot on their minds, though. They're contemplating the feasibility of extending network television facilities to Albuquerque, New Mexico. Albuquerque's the only major city in the country this year of our Lord 1952 with a TV station that does not have a network tie-in. Long Lines can either come up from the south or down from the north, via coaxial cable or microwave radio relay. In either case the cost is not prohibitive, but considered from an economic standpoint or a practical standpoint as to covering the country with a spider web of TV coverage, it is not definitely *feasible*. The kicker is that the Albuquerque station is owned jointly by a former chief commissioner of the Federal Communications Commission and by Time-Life Corporation. If AT&T Long Lines knows which side of the bread to butter—well, then. . . .

There's a dry-cleaning price war in Memphis. Loeb Laundry Cleaners will clean dresses for 50¢, men's suits for 45¢, skirts and blouses for 25¢—half-price down the line. This has upset the rest of the cleaners in Memphis. They took space in the *Memphis Press-Scimitar* for an open letter to Mr. William Loeb and Mr. Henry Loeb: "Dear Bill and Henry: . . . You both have proved that you believe in fair play—and, Henry, you took that issue into the recent American Legion election—and WON." The gist of their grievance is that "the present cut prices are far below our actual production costs. So, Bill and Henry, all we and the public want to know is, WHY?"

I think the public probably already knows why and is happy enough with the answer.

Dynamite told me about a farmer who came up to him while he was sitting in his truck to complain that Bell trucks were making his cows nervous and their milk production was falling off—and just then a cow stuck its head through the window of the cab and looked contentedly at both of them. And about another farmer who charged them $5.00 to let Ma Bell's truck on his land. That night the splicer called and said the gate was padlocked. Cost Ma Bell another $5.00 to get her truck off the farmer's land.

Over in Tennessee a candidate for governor is being charged with avoiding overseas service and his accuser is being charged with being liable to arrest in Alabama for smuggling liquor. At the Democratic convention in Chicago, Senator Estes Kefauver—the overwhelming people's choice in the primaries—was allotted 30 seats for visitors from Tennessee, while Governor Adlai Stevenson of Illinois got 700 for visitors from Illinois. Guess which candidate the Democratic National Committee wanted to see a big demonstration for.

I spent last weekend in Memphis. On the cabbie's recommendation, I stayed at the Peabody, an old, and honored, hotel there. On the menus in the Peabody's restaurant are printed the first few bars of "Dixie." When originally printed, long ago, there was a mistake in the musical notation. This mistake has been retained and is now a hallowed southern tradition. No mention on the Peabody's historical menu about the armed whites who in 1866 burned down every black church in Memphis and killed 40 blacks while doing it. There's probably at least one very old black here right now who was a tiny baby when it happened. Southern traditions. Southern history.

Cab driver told me, "Memphis is a clean city, an' friendly, too. You got any questions, you just ask 'em of anyone on the street, they'll be glad to he'p you." Cabbies in Memphis will not, as a rule, pick up Negroes, especially at night. They say they've been hijacked too often. "Thass our only trouble down here," my cab driver explained, "the niggers. They are niggers, too. They're illiterate, can't read or write, and they get to thinkin' someone's pushin' them around." He raised his voice. "One of 'em gets outta line, though, we work him over and that's all she wrote!" Tells me about the Prairie Schooner tour and the Cave and in West Memphis the Plantation Club and the Cotton Club.

The Prairie Schooner turns out to be a two-bit boat that makes a quick turn around Mud Island and you get to see Mississippi mud, Negroes on the river bank tending their trot lines, a dredger in action, and some oil-pumping stations. For $1.00 for an advertised hour tour that goes less than 45 minutes it is the dullest way to spend time in Memphis. And that's saying something for Beale Street city.

The Cave looks like a cave and smells like a cave but acts like a high school rec room. It's a hangout for hundreds of sailors just out of boot camp who are stationed at a base outside of Memphis. It's a dump but the proprietor will sell beer to underage boys and buy whiskey for them, so it's a popular liberty hangout. Six years ago I'd have been here enjoying it myself.

I found a good place to eat in Memphis: Jimmie and Pappie's, way out from the center of town. Big old boy comes slamming in and bangs on the table with a new fifth to order for his foursome. The big guy orders lobsters as an opener, then two-pound steaks. Offers to bet me $100 Adlai would beat Eisenhower. But the two women in the party say

Stevenson is Truman's tool and Ike will win. The women's eyes are glittering from the booze and their skin is a dark, dark, leathery brown, like they'd been to Miami for a 40-day burn.

On Monday we finish early and T. Tom tells about his weekend. T. Tom is a master splicer and proud of his skills, and he's feisty. ("I'm easy to fuck the first time, but the second time—watch out!") He thinks Dynamite is too bossy, says he's going to bring in a loaf of white bread for Dynamite to chew on, so he can leave off chewing on the crew.

T. Tom is always being picked up by girls in a bar. This past weekend it happened to him again, but guess what—the woman had three breasts! Looked normal enough under a brassiere, he says, but there they were. "I've seen plenty of six-teated cows," he says, "but never a three-teated woman."

T. Tom related how on one six-week assignment for Ma Bell he spent only two actual days on the job, rest of the time in the sack. Would go out, tell the crew what to do, return to the motel. "I dressed and undressed that girl for her dates," he says.

Today one of Forrest City's most polite, courtly merchants tried to short-change me half a buck when I bought a workshirt. What a surprise to him when his error was pointed out. They overcharge you in the cafes, too and give you dry sandwiches with a thin slice of meat and sour cream for your coffee.

There is an ancient, falling-down Lincoln School here for Negroes. It's vacation time for the whites but Negro kids get to go to school now because when cotton-picking time comes they will have to be in the fields. But you can't pick no cotton if the cotton's rotten, can you? At the Forrest City hospital—one of them, maybe it was just a clinic—the Colored Waiting Room is: "TO THE REAR, UPSTAIRS." There's an outside wooden stairway to the second floor; you're in trouble if you're too sick or banged-up to climb stairs, I guess.

Sixty-three days now without rain. Reached 107° F. yesterday. The Baptists are building a brand-new, huge church. It will cover in two wings most of a block. The Negro Baptist church building is a wreck.

I talked to a white farmer who remembers the Depression. In 1931 he and his daddy had a "little old sawmill" on an acreage the bank foreclosed on and he went to work cutting ditches at 35¢ an hour. He laughs about a "Hoover Dust" cheap tobacco he smoked then, and of eating rabbit, which was considered edible only in winter but "Hoover made rabbit good in the summertime." I ask him about Eisenhower. "I've got sense enough to know Hoover probably wasn't responsible," he says, "but when I think about those times I just can't bring myself to vote Republican."

When I was waiting on the Clarks' just-poor-country-folks porch last Friday for the cab to take me to the bus depot to get into Memphis

(40 miles as Jim Crow flies), Mrs. Clark kept me company. Sipping at a glass of lemonade, she was telling what a pity it was the black kids didn't learn their three R's. "Poor things," she said, "but they don't even care enough to go to school."

I had a light bag with a change of clothes and my razor and toothbrush in it. When the cab pulled up in front and the black cabbie got out and looked up the walk at us, I bent down to pick up the bag. Mrs. Clark put her free hand on my arm and said into my ear, pretty fiercely for such a sugar-toned woman, "Make him come and get it!"

When I left the Peabody to come back to Forrest City the desk clerk was chewing out a bellboy, very black, maybe 14 or 15 years old, who stood there grinning and embarrassed. The day before I'd watched the kid stagger away from the desk with four suitcases and instructions to climb two flights of stairs to a guest's room. "It's not everybody who gets a chance to work in a hotel like this and have it so easy," the desk clerk was saying. "Now you better wake up or by God you know what I'm gonna do? I'm gonna take a stick to your scalp."

The greyhounds burn kerosene in this part of the country. Last Sunday a bus carrying 34 Memphis Baptists home from an assembly at Ridgecrest, North Carolina, exploded and burned in a high gap of the Smokies just after the group stopped and got out for prayer. Twelve Baptists were hospitalized with burns. But what if they hadn't stopped to pray?

T. Tom told about one time on a Sunday he was caught in a woman's house when her boyfriend arrived. T. Tom said he kicked his shorts under the bed, pulled on his pants, and pretended he was working on the telephone. (His truck was outside at the curb.) Called the operator, got a test line, went through the rigamarole. Back at his motel he was complimenting himself on his escape and the phone rings. Man says, "I just want you to know I know you weren't testing any phone."

Prindle usually doesn't say much, but this time he counters with a story about one time he was hauled drunk and laughing into a Texas jail. In the same room a cop is beating the beejesus out of a Negro. Negro is bleeding bad, rocking his head in his hands. Cop says, "Don't you get any of that blood on the floor." Negro sways dizzily and a drop of his blood falls to the floor. Cop begins beating on the Negro again, harder than before. Prindle says, "I stopped laughing. I was next in line."

When I went into Memphis last weekend and was getting off the bus a little white girl about five or six ahead of me says, "Last one off's a nigger-baby." Her mother yanks her by the arm. "Now you've opened your mouth just once too often," her mother says. "What if there's one of them waiting outside to get you right now?"

What if.

Cornelius Vanderbilt (1794-1877)
Steamship and railroad owner
(Engraving by A. H. Ritchie)

Washington Duke (1820-1905)
Cigarette manufacturer
(Duke University)

John D. Rockefeller (1839-1937)
Oil magnate
(Library of Congress)

J. P. Morgan (1837-1913)
Financier
(Library of Congress)

Eminent Opinions

The modern capitalist looks upon life as a financial combat of a very specialized kind, regulated by a code which he understands and has indeed himself concocted, but which is recognized by no one else in the world. He conceives sovereign powers to be for sale. He may, he thinks, buy them; and if he buys them, he may use them as he pleases. He believes, for instance, that it is the lawful, nay more! in America, that it is the constitutional right of the citizen to buy the national highways, and, having bought them, to use them as a common carrier might use a horse and cart upon a public road. He may sell his service to whom he pleases at what price may suit him, and if by doing so he ruins men and cities, it is nothing to him. He is not responsible, for he is not a trustee for the public. . . .

. . . If the capitalist has bought some sovereign function, and wishes to abuse it for his own behoof, he regards the law which restrains him as a despotic invasion of his constitutional rights, because, with his specialized mind, he cannot grasp the relation of a sovereign function to the nation as a whole. He, therefore, looks upon the evasion of a law devised for public protection, but inimical to him, as innocent or even meritorious.

If an election be lost, and the legislature, which has been chosen by the majority, cannot be pacified by money, but passes some act which promises to be annoying, the first instinct of the capitalist is to retain counsel, not to advise him touching his duty under the law, but to devise a method by which he may elude it, or, if he cannot elude it, by which he may have it annulled as unconstitutional by the courts. The lawyer who succeeds in this branch of practice is certain to win the highest prizes at the bar. . . .

The foregoing words and the thoughts they express were published in 1913 by Brooks Adams, a noted American historian. They are included here to show that the excesses and tendencies of the Gilded Age did not go unremarked by contemporary social observers.

For that matter, three-quarters of a century earlier a 28-year-old Abraham Lincoln had commented on the same type of man scrutinized by Adams, saying, "These capitalists generally act harmoniously, and in concert, to fleece the public."

If this book has among its readers some of this country's youth, it is possible that their rejoinder to the inclusion of Adams' comments and Lincoln's would be, "Ancient history, man. Who cares?" (Though if that is their attitude, they're not reading this book at all, are they.)

Well, of course, Adams and Lincoln *are* becoming ancient history. Given enough time, everyone and everything does, I suppose. But I have noticed that many of the younger members of our body politic seem to glory in their excessive ignorance of any event or thought that preceded their own birth. For example, they do not know when our military forces were engaged in Vietnam, or Korea, or when World War II took place, much less World War I. As for the Spanish-American War, all of the Indian wars, the Civil War, the War with Mexico, the War of 1812, or the American Revolutionary War, for many of our youngest citizens these conflicts exist in an almost prehistoric haze. And of the few who can place our nation's major armed conflicts in time, most have only vague notions of why we went to war when we did, or what happened after.

This is true, also, with respect to less bloody events and movements and moments of consequence in our history. All that many of the young seem to be able to muster about such matters is, indifferently, "That's bull crap, man."

Much of it is. But why is it? How is it? And what can we learn to our benefit from answers to those questions?

The young's acceptance of ignorance—a prideful acceptance—is not going to help them avoid piling it higher and deeper in their own lives. It may be said that a saving grace of nonfatal mistakes is that we can learn from them—but only if we know what the mistake was all about, its details, its causes, and its results.

I have a friend, also an old fogey, who tells me I expect too much, that today's further instances of the enormous condescension of posterity are not to be wondered at or censured.

I don't think so. I don't expect any more from or for the young than they of themselves, which is to gain an inkling of what they're living their lives for, a question universally asked by man, if not explicitly, then implicitly, especially when he/she is young. But to get a glimmer of an answer to this question (besides the obvious: to pass on a packet of genes), you have to furnish your mind, so to speak, with lumber to work on.

Brooks Adams in the passages quoted has some few words to say about lawyers. Louis Dembitz Brandeis, a distinguished jurist (assoc. justice, U.S. Supreme Court, 1916-39), in a speech he gave in 1905 also had words for lawyers:

It is true that at the present time the lawyer does not hold as high a position with the people as he held seventy-five or indeed fifty years ago; but the reason is not lack of opportunity. It is this: Instead of holding a position of independence, between the wealthy and the people, prepared to curb the excesses of either, able lawyers have, to a large extent, allowed themselves to become adjuncts of great corporations and have neglected the obligation to use their powers for the protection of the people. We hear much of the "corporation lawyer," and far too little of the "people's lawyer." The great opportunity of the American bar is and will be to stand again as it did in the past, ready to protect also the interests of the people. . . .

The leading lawyers of the United States have been engaged mainly in supporting the claims of the corporations; often in endeavoring to evade or nullify the extremely crude laws by which legislators sought to regulate the power or curb the excesses of corporations.

Such questions as the regulation of trusts, the fixing of railway rates, the municipalization of public utilities, the relation between capital and labor, call for the exercise of legal ability of the highest order. Up to the present time the legal ability of a high order which has been expended on those questions has been almost wholly in opposition to the contentions of the people. The leaders of the bar, without any preconceived intent on their part, and rather as an incident to their professional standing, have, with rare exceptions, been ranged on the side of the corporations, and the people have been represented, in the main, by men of very meager legal ability.

If these problems are to be settled right, this condition cannot continue. Our country is, after all, not a country of dollars, but of ballots. The immense corporate wealth will necessarily develop a hostility from which much trouble will come to us unless the excesses of capital are curbed, through the respect for law, as the excesses of democracy were curbed seventy-five years ago. There will come a revolt of the people against the capitalists, unless the aspirations of the people are given some adequate legal expression; and to this end cooperation of abler lawyers is essential.

For nearly a generation the leaders of the bar have, with

few exceptions, not only failed to take part in constructive legislation designed to solve in the public interest our great social, economic and industrial problems; but, they have failed likewise to oppose legislation prompted by selfish interests. They have often gone further in disregard of common weal. They have often advocated, as lawyers, legislative measures which as citizens they could not approve, and have endeavored to justify themselves by a false analogy. They have erroneously assumed that the rule of ethics to be applied to a lawyer's advocacy is the same where he acts for private interests against the public, as it is in litigation between private individuals.

Justice Brandeis was born the year the Civil War Ended. He died the year the United States entered World War II. Ninety years ago, as we have seen, he gave as his opinion that "If these problems are to be settled right, this condition cannot continue." He was referring to the exercise of corporate power at the expense of the public. Of course, the condition has not only continued, it has grown at an almost geometric rate of progression. And continues to do so even to this very day. Perhaps, as Brandeis said, "much trouble will come to us."

Honest Injun

Neither the American colonies nor the United States government ever honored a treaty they made with the Native Americans. Not one.

In 1891 an old Indian—veteran of many treaty councils—summarized this situation: "They made us many promises, more than I can remember, but they never kept but one; they promised to take our land and they took it."

Nicodemus

In the late 1980s the English social documentarian, Tony Parker (Studs Terkel would be our equivalent), was interviewing the residents of a small town, population 2,000, in Kansas, smack-dab in the middle of America.

Parker gave the name "Bird" to the small town in which for 3½ months he talked to people, and his interviews were published in 1989 in a most excellent book titled *A Place Called Bird*.

The residents of this ordinary, everyday, small town on the fringe of the Bible Belt are ordinary, everyday, small-town Americans, with only a very few Winesburg, Ohio, grotesqueries. Protestants for the most part—friendly, easy-going, decent, honest, upright, tidy. Bird sits on a flat prairie under a vast arch of blue most days, a million stars at night.

Bird has one feature that sets it off from other small towns in Kansas: Nicodemus, a settlement on the Solomon River of about 75 people who are virtual strangers to the residents of Bird.

Here is how the student counselor at Bird's high school brought up Nicodemus with Parker:

There's maybe one important thing though I think we haven't come to grips with yet here, and that's the subject of colour. Just along the road down at Nicodemus there's an all-black settlement, where the people are descendants of negro slaves. OK they keep themselves to themselves a lot: you don't see many of them coming into town here to do their shopping and so on, and very few of their kids either. We don't have a single black child in our High School for example. I think the people of Bird are happy to let it go along like that, as though Nicodemus wasn't anything to do with us: I'd go further and say as though black people altogether weren't anything to do with us, even if they are only just a few miles away. This worries me, this situation where

73

people seem to pretend Nicodemus doesn't exist, and if we don't think about it perhaps it'll go away. I had a parent only the other day, to all extent otherwise a reasonably intelligent well-educated person, who told me quite seriously 'Do you know, in all my life I've never met a black person and I wouldn't want to. Not because I'm colour prejudiced or anything, because I'm not: it's just I don't like black people, that's all.' And I'm sorry to say this but I think it's true: I think what she said's true of a lot of people here.

In the 92 interviews of residents of Bird and nearby Garland included in Parker's book, this and another, passing, reference are the only mentions of the existence of Nicodemus; 289 pages of extensive interviews, of conversations that range over everything under the sun—except Nicodemus.

A fair-haired, blue-eyed housewife in Bird said to Parker:

Caucasians, whites, they take themselves as normal: if you marry into a different race like I did, they're not sure how to treat you. They somehow can't talk easily with you. I notice this more because I was born and grew up here: everyone used to be at ease and friendly with me. Now I'm a white woman married to a Red Indian and with two children: and to them now, that's something else. Through Pete and what he's told me and we've talked about, I've got books to read about: so now I know much better about the Indians and their way of life and how we exploited them. But if you talk about it, it's real funny how uppity some white people get. Only just a few weeks back, I'd been in Gover's and when I came out there was a woman I knew on Main and we visited a while. We got around to talking about east Kansas, the land round there, and I said something like how originally it'd been Indian territory and we'd stolen it from them. I didn't mean nothing by it, I was just making a comment. But she looked real mad, she said 'Well you can't blame me and my generation for that, none of us was even born when that happened!' . . .

Her husband intervenes:

What I am is a White Mountain Apache Indian: my people originally came from the Rocky Mountain area in Colorado. There's an Apache reservation in Arizona, but that's desert land and it's not where we really belong. It's the white man designated it as belonging to us, like the whites do in South Africa: they take a land that's not rich and call it a tribal homeland and send people there. It was the same here with us. They took the land where we

74

were originally away from us, signed treaties with us to say we'd sold it to them, and then afterwards told us we couldn't go there any more. But buying land, owning it, that was a white man's concept, not an Indian's: to Indian people no one could anymore own the earth than they could the sky. They gave us one of three choices: to migrate and go away, to stay there and adapt to white ways, or to perish. Only you know this isn't a subject you find a lot of folk want to talk about, not in a small town like this: or anywhere else much either.

Later in the conversation his wife remarks, "People are just people," to which he responds, "Sure, I know that and you know that. But they don't: there's their kind of people and there's other kinds of people: they're happy with one kind and one kind only, which is their own."

A visiting professor of history, Christine Peach, from the University of Texas at Houston is the first interviewee to talk about Nicodemus at length. For six years Professor Peach has been working on an extended study of the architecture and history of Nicodemus and other Negro settlements. "I don't know how you've found the people of Bird with regard to Nicodemus," she says,

a white experience of whites can't be the same as a black person's, but for myself when I go there, maybe once or twice in a week to the library, I feel there's a very definite, almost so positive kind of indifference you almost touch it. We may be only ten miles apart along the road, but very few people there seem to have any sense we're neighbouring communities. Nicodemus could be 1,000 miles and 1,000 years away for all the thought they give it.

In a way I find that infinitely depressing. Bird turns its back on Nicodemus and pretends it isn't there and it isn't happening, the same as it does with a lot of other things. That's small town typical, I guess. And Nicodemus turns its back on Bird too, you have to say that, here's just as much an inward-looking community. Only if you happen to believe like I do, that the only solution to the problem of race relations is complete integration—the opposite being complete and total separation, which like in South Africa becomes total dynamite—well then it's hard to see how and when and where this coming together is to occur. There's not a sign even the thought of it exists, not in a place like Bird: and how you'd begin with it is not something you can even see starting to happen. Now that *is* depressing: in the heartland of America there's no sign of progress at all in such a vitally important area of human relationships.

Professor Peach is black and staying in a house in Nicodemus. She gains Parker an entree to other residents of Nicodemus and he interviews seven. (One of his interviewees begins their conversation by saying, "Well you know it's nice having you visit me, I don't recall in all my life I've ever had a white man sitting in my kitchen before.") Here is a comment from an 82-year-old man:

My daddy, he stayed here the whole of his life because he hoped one day that piece of land would be his: and so did I, I stayed here all my life with the same hope too. But sometime around what they called the depression years, things got so bad we had to sell our land to the big landowners in Kansas City Missoura: and ever since then, all we've had was the renting of it to work on but never again to own. That landowner he was a white man, of course he was: and in that story is the story of how things have always been between the white man and the black man.

I'm a hard-working man and I have been all my life: I'm as poor as Job's turkey but so long as I can work I'm happy, and I've four of my children living here in Demus working the land. I go along every day I can do and I work with them too. . . .

. . . I'd like to have been able to say least I'd been one time out of Kansas, but I can't. On the television you see some mighty fine places: you say to yourself you'd like to visit them if you had the money you could afford it. But I think if you think too much like that, after a while you only make yourself unhappy. So I remind myself of all the blessings I've had in my life, and all the happinesses the Good Lord has showered on me: my mammy and daddy, our good home, my pretty wife Laura, our children, everything. It's been more than any one man deserves: but like it tells you in the Bible, if you're a servant to God and carry out His will and don't complain, He'll be storing up treasure for you in Heaven, and when you go to Him there, you'll get your reward.

And from a 65-year-old man:

I don't wait till they came for me, I went to them. I could offer certain skills I'd picked up like a knowledge of automobiles, and before long found myself chauffeur to a General, which was a very fine job. He was one of those who carried on the war from his desk in the Pentagon most of the time, and was very very careful not to do anything foolish like letting himself be sent either across the Atlantic or across the Pacific near where any fighting was. He was an able man, and a wise one was that General: and I was happy to chauffeur him anywhere he wanted to go across the continent of North America. It was an arrangement suited me like it suited him. Doing that sort of an occupation you know, that meant I did, I continued to have some very good times. . . .

And children yes certainly as well: there were many of those, and they were always a great joy. More wives and children than I can exactly remember you know. There are nine children of mine I know of who come regularly to visit their daddy, and always I'm very happy to see them. Five of them live here in Nicodemus, three girls and two boys: they've all grown into fine people, four of them now married themselves. And there's not one of them whose home I'm not welcome in: now that's a proud thing for a man to be able to say, in these times when you're hearing so much everywhere about the breaking up of families and divorce.

I thank the Lord for giving me such a good and happy life. All my pleasures have been the simple delights of loving and laughing, most particularly with the ladies: I've had so many good times, I really have, times beyond number most every place I've been.

And from a man 45 years old, sitting on the back steps of his house, tired and dusty from the day's work:

One of my sisters that was in Nicodemus here, she told us of this house we could have for next to nothing: the man who it had belonged to had died, his wife had gone back to Kentucky and she was more concerned not to have it to look after than to get a price for it. So we borrowed some money and bought it and we moved in, and we've been here ever since. From that day to this I've never had a good job with good money ever: but from that day to this also, I've never had one single day I was out of work. each week we always had enough to get by on, or a little less, even if we never had a whole lot more. But the children have been fed and they've growed up into three fine young ladies: one of them's married and gone to California, one of them's married and living in Conway City, and the youngest one you can hear now cooking in the kitchen there for our supper.

There's one big sadness though: it's like there always is in life for everyone, joy and sorrow. Two years ago now my wife was taken into hospital with cancer: they found it too late to do anything that could save her, and she died two weeks to the day from when they took her in. Only still a young woman, 45 years of age: and if you'd have seen her she looked as young and as well as the day I first met her. It takes a time for a person to find a purpose in life again when someone's taken away as sudden as that. It's difficult to see how I will, especially when our baby here goes off as she will in her time. I'll go on working because that's the only way of life I know now, but I couldn't tell you at my age who it'd be for. I come home here after a day's work on a warm summer's evening like this, and it seems living's got no purpose to it any more. Maybe the Lord'll take a hand again, and step in again to show me a way.

From a 44-year-old woman who works at a home for old white people, who do not always treat her well, who accuse her of stealing from them, of being a prostitute:

I'd like it if I were able to go to the lady in charge and tell her I don't have to take that sort of treatment, I'll go work some place else. But I do have to take it: someone who's not got no education like me, they have to work and be thankful they have any kind of a job.

You'll hear tell these days there ain't prejudice against black people just on account of them being black, there ain't that kind of prejudice anywhere no more: because it's illegal and against the law. But you can't pass laws that are going to stop people being rude to you, and saying things against the colour of your skin like they do. My children, they all go to school in Deerfield, and they sure get plenty things said to them there. There's teachers who tell them they're lazy and slow with their work and say that's how all blacks are, and things of that sort. I tell them pay no attention and work hard, so that one day they'll maybe be like that Mrs Peach lady: they'll be the ones who're clever and they'll have white pupils who have to set listening to them.

It's sad there's all this prejudice still, one person not liking another and only for because they're black. I don't know why all people can't live on earth together friendly like the Lord said they should. . . .

From a 17-year-old girl:

My school's OK but some of the teachers there, they have a down on black kids: it makes it sometimes you feel you can't get away from it soon enough when you grow up. There's one they call your careers adviser: and every black girl goes to talk with her, she tells them all exactly the selfsame thing. She says there's lots of good jobs for smart black girls in supermarkets and restaurants if they work hard: she says the trouble with black folk is that they most of them don't want to work, so anyone who does they can do OK. White girls, she encourages them to think of going to college and learning for a proper career: but I've talked with my friends, and I've not known one black girl she's ever said to anything like that. If that's how she feels about black people I don't think she should be the person to advise them. . . .

. . . But you get prejudice worse from the other pupils, specially where it's the boys. Right now there's a white boy there, he's a senior, and he's always telling everyone how he's scored with every one of the black girls there is in the school. It's not true and he gives black girls a bad reputation. He's all the time boasting, and then some of the other white boys come whispering behind your back and calling you black trash. I'd never go with no white boy myself ever, not now or the rest of my life. I think the whites should stay with the whites and the blacks with the blacks. There was a girl at our school and she and her white boy friend, they loved each other and wanted to get married: but the boy's ma and pa, they said they weren't having their son marrying no black girl, and they wouldn't let him take her to their home not once.

I don't see how white people and black people are ever going to get together in a country like America, where those who are white have all the things and keep them for themselves. I don't know what it's like in other places because I've not been nowhere else, but you see programmes on television about other countries: and wherever you look, you see black people who are poor. . . .

And, finally, from a college-educated woman in her early 50s who for 12 years has been the personnel manager of an agricultural supply firm in Conway City that has a large black work force:

I hate all white people. I won't say to you that it's not a thing against you personally, because that wouldn't be true. It is against you personally, as it is to any black man or black woman when a white person insults them or demeans them or mistreats them. This is something whites don't know, or don't choose to know: that when you strike at a person because of their race or the colour of their skin, you're doing it to them as an individual and they feel the hurt as an individual. They might protest it afterwards and say it was done to them because they were black: but that's to cover the hurt that's been done to them as a person. Unless you've had it happen to you, I don't think you could understand it. The black people are seen as being without individual personalities by whites but that's not how they see themselves.

It will take another great leader to teach them that: Dr. Martin Luther King was beginning to help them feel they had worth and needn't for ever be slaves. But those who killed him, and I'm one of many many thousands who think his assassination was planned by a group of people and not the responsibility of one crazy man, they planted such bitterness by that in black people's hearts it'll take a hundred years or more for it to go. . . . The lesson of it for many black people will be this: that for their next leader, he'll take them further only if he offers them their rights not in some future dreamtime, but now. If he tells them they mustn't wait any longer for their rights to be given them but must take them now, that will be a time we've not so far seen the like of ever in America. There won't be just street riots and damage to property, there'll be killings and burnings and terrorising and worse things still, beyond imagining. I'm speaking now not of what I'm advocating but what I fear: difficult though it is to be, myself I'm a pacifist and I don't want to see black justice come through the injustice of force. . . .

You get to hear in the job all kinds of problems people have: they like to come and talk with you about things nothing to do with work but in their personal or family lives. All of that too reinforces the view you have of the life of black people and how they're disadvantaged. You'll have heard around these parts of oil being found? But on black man's land, the companies aren't even yet drilling looking for it. . . . I've not known of a single case where a black man's profited from oil, not anywhere near here at all. Such things as that, they all add to the picture of two classes of citizens, the first-class whites and the second-class blacks.

All right. But you want to know how the mayor of the town of Bird itself sees it?

The way I see it? OK well I'll tell you. The way I see it is that America's just the greatest little country that there is. Whatever you want, America has it, right here. A fine, freedom-loving country, democracy, free speech, freedom of religion, everything. And you know what the greatest freedom of all is? Well let me tell you: it's freedom of opportunity. A man wants to improve himself, make his way in the world by his hard work and his efforts, and he'll do that: if he works hard and lives a decent kind of a life, there's no limit to where he can get to, right up to one day becoming the President of the United States if that's what he's got a mind to. You only need look back through the history books, and it's all there, how the ordinary men and the women too for that matter, if they worked and had the determination to succeed, then there wasn't no one could stop them. . . .

80

The Jolly Roger

At the turn of the last century, President Theodore Roosevelt—one of the four Presidential faces blasted out of Mt. Rushmore—expressed an American vision that has guided our leaders ever since. Progress, Roosevelt said, is "due solely to the power of the mighty civilized races which have not lost the fighting instinct, and which by their expansion are gradually bringing peace to the red wastes where the barbarian peoples of the world hold sway."

By "mighty civilized races" Theodore Roosevelt meant the white race, his own race. By "barbarian peoples" he meant anyone who was not of his color. Theodore Roosevelt's big-stick foreign policy made the Caribbean safe for U.S. dollar diplomacy and United Fruit. It gave us the Panama Canal and earned the enmity of Central America and much of South America. Theodore Roosevelt was an imperialist. The military expeditions he sent into the Philippines against the Moros after the Spanish-American War, were themselves barbaric, like all colonial wars. An American soldier there reported that "We never left one alive. If one was wounded, we would run our bayonets through them."

A hundred and thirty years before the slaughter of the Moros, the first American patriot casualty in the American Revolution was the escaped slave—part Indian, part black—Crispus Attucks, killed by British troops in Boston on March 5, 1770. (As it happened, six years later Jefferson drafted a paragraph for the Declaration of Independence condemning slavery; the rest of the drafting committee deleted it.) Washington had his slaves freed upon his death because of the respect he had gained for the black soldiers who fought under him in the Revolutionary War.

In the Civil War, a total of 178,000 black soldiers and 30,000 black sailors fought with the Union (93,000 from the seceded states), and at least 38,000 lost their lives in the conflict. (Blacks in the Union military were paid $7.00 a month; whites got $13.00.) Still, in the North, white mobs, believing they were being drafted to liberate blacks who would take their jobs, rioted in New York, Boston, Albany, Cleveland, Detroit, and Chicago, killing hundreds of Negroes and burning their homes and shops.

In the late 19th-century Indian Wars, white officers vied to command black troops because of the blacks' superior performance in the "Buffalo Soldier" campaigns. The same was true in Cuba in the Spanish-American War.

During World War I, some 200,000 black troops served overseas, 50,000 in combat. The first American soldier in WW I to win France's highest military award, the Croix de Guerre (his with star and palm) was Sergeant Henry Johnson, a Pullman porter in civilian life. The 369th Infantry Regiment of the American Expeditionary Force was one of the AEF's racially segregated black units (white officers, black enlisted men). The 369th spent 191 days under fire, didn't give up a foot of ground to the Boche. It, too, won the Croix de Guerre. (General "Black Jack" Pershing, commander of the AEF, got his nickname from the segregated troops he commanded on a punitive expedition into Mexico in 1916. Earlier in his career he had commanded the troops that put down the Moro uprisings.)

Altogether, 370,000 African-Americans served in U.S. armed forces in WW I, a war fought, according to then President Wilson, "to make the world safe for democracy." Woodrow Wilson was a Southern Democrat, born in Virginia. He told "darky" stories in Cabinet meetings and the officials of his administration systematically segregated government offices and restrooms for the first time since the Civil War. The initial impetus for this policy came from Wilson's wife who was horrified, when given a tour of the Bureau of Printing and Engraving, to see blacks and whites working side by side. (She also detested suffragettes—women who campaigned for the vote.)

Despite his idealistic public pronouncements, Woodrow Wilson was a racist. His vision was blurred by bigotry. (At the peace treaty conference after WW I he ignored a young Ho Chi Minh who asked for self-determination for his country. The reverberations of Wilson's rebuff of the young patriot returned to devastate the United States half a century later.)

In the first year following the end of WW I, there were 83 lynchings in the United States, several of blacks still in uniform, some of whom were burned alive. The Ku Klux Klan held more than 200 public meetings in 1919 from New England to Indiana to Florida, and there were 25 major race riots within a few months of each other. In Chicago's 1919 race riot, 23 Negroes were killed, 600 wounded, and 1,000 families were burned out of their homes. In Omaha, Nebraska, a Negro was dragged through the streets, shot more than a thousand times, and then his corpse was hanged on Omaha's main street.

In World War II, more than a million black men and women wore military uniforms, the same uniforms as those that whites wore but the blacks' duties and their units were segregated. Black U.S. infantry divisions saw hard fighting and suffered severe casualties in both the European and Pacific theaters of operation, most notably the 92nd in Italy, the 93rd in the Pacific. Few Americans at home learned of it. (The same happened to Japanese-American soldiers.)

On the home front during WW II, German prisoners in transit could dine in southern railway stations but their black American guards could not. Black soldiers on furlough could not get home if the Jim Crow coach on an otherwise half-empty train was filled. Bombings, arson, and forced evictions were frequent in the North, where blacks were moving to defense jobs, and race riots broke out in many northern and southern cities all during the war.

At war's end, Mississippi Governor Fielding L. Wright went on the radio to "advise" the Negroes of his state that if they contemplated social equality and the sharing of school, hotel, and restaurant facilities with whites, they should "make your home in some other state than Mississippi." In Georgia, the Ku Klux Klan had its biggest membership surge since the '20s, celebrating with a mammoth cross-burning outside of Atlanta. Fifty miles east of Atlanta there was a horrific quadruple lynching.

Only now, in 1996, has the Pentagon sent to the President the names of seven WW II black servicemen as nominees for the Medal of Honor. Six of the seven are dead.

Some time after the middle of the 20th century—in the early 1960s—an overwhelming urge to fight in Asia seized our national leaders and we began sending U.S. troops to Vietnam. *Something* seized our leaders then, though to this day no one has pinned down exactly what. A paroxysm of the fighting instinct, perhaps, or John Wayne machismo. Once there, our troops killed three million Vietnamese and 58,000 of our own were killed, thousands more maimed in mind and body. Our combat troops called enemy territory "Injun country," perhaps having in mind the much admired 1869 opinion of Civil War general Phil Sheridan that, "The only good Indian is a dead Indian."

During our prolonged stay in Vietnam a U.S. Army officer provided an oblique summary of what we were accomplishing: "It became necessary," he said after one engagement, "to destroy the town to save it." The officer's statement is a supreme example of the functioning of the serious military mind.

The number of Asian men, women, and children we murdered half a world away in Vietnam, and the disparity between our own losses and theirs, might have shamed Attila the Hun or Genghis Khan, though it had no such effect on the best and brightest of the U.S. global strategists who ordered the mass killings, all men beyond combat age themselves or excused from the fighting by virtue of their superior intellects and worth to the nation. (At that, our casualties in Vietnam were only 4,000 more than the 54,000 U.S. troops killed in Korea, 1950-1953, in a quarter of the time. A total of 4.4 million humans were killed in the Korean War, both sides, civilian and military.)

> I pray you to pause and consider. Against our traditions we are now entering upon an unjust and trivial war, a war against a helpless people, and for a base object—robbery. . . . To be a patriot, one had to say, and keep on saying, "Our Country, right or wrong," and urge on the little war. . . . The stupid phrase needed help, and it got another one: "Even if the war be wrong we are in it and must fight it out: *we cannot retire from it without dishonor.*" Why, not even a burglar could have said it better. . . .

Thus Mark Twain indicted the U.S. war in the Philippines against the Moros. Does anyone doubt he would have said the same about the U.S. war against Vietnam's Viet Cong? Because of American atrocities in the Philippines, Twain proposed that the white stripes in the U.S. flag be painted black and the stars on their field of blue be replaced by a skull and crossbones. Academic literary scholars have been very successful in ignoring this facet of the work of the father of American prose.

A statement made in a *New York Times* interview in 1931 by a retired Marine Corps general, Smedley Butler, gives some perspective on U.S. foreign policy and our military actions supporting it:

> "I helped make Mexico safe for American oil interests in 1914. I helped make Haiti and Cuba a decent place for the National City Bank boys to collect revenue in. I helped purify Nicaragua for the international banking house of Brown Brothers. . . . I brought light to the Dominican Republic for American sugar interests in 1916. I helped make Honduras 'right' for American fruit companies in 1903. Looking back on it, I might have given Al Capone a few hints."

Butler didn't live to see us help install the Shah in Iran in 1953, or the U.S. role in bringing down the elected government of Guatemala in 1954, or our rigging of the 1957 election in Lebanon, or our role in the assassination of Patrice Lumumba of the Congo (later Zaire) in 1961, or our repeated attempts to assassinate Premier Fidel Castro of Cuba, or our involvement in overthrowing the elected government of Chile in 1973, or any of our more recent piratical diddlings in Grenada, Panama,

Nicaragua, and the Middle East, or any of half a dozen other murderous meddlings in the affairs of other nations.

The wealthy of this country have never been hesitant to use American power to interfere with the politics of other countries in which they have an economic stake. This is done in the name of furthering democracy throughout the world, yet we usually find ourselves—surprise!—shoring up dictators who will support American business interests.

Usually, the rich have our adversaries picked with great care, but their minions failed them when they chose Vietnam. It was a profound blow to our national pride when we had to flee that small country, defeated by the Viet Cong of Ho Chi Minh.

The 12-year Vietnam War formally ended on January 27, 1973. Its direct cost in dollars to America was $110 billion. It was fought by a disproportionate number of poor and jobless black Americans. White middle-class youths managed, as often as not, to avoid the draft. The enlisted men who fought the Vietnam War were poor blacks and whites, for the most part, their officers were the professional military. Whites from the South were heavily represented among the poor whites and officers—and there was black-and-white conflict in the U.S. military throughout the war.

During the war, Muhammad Ali, heavyweight boxing champion of the world in the 1960s, was drafted but refused induction to the U.S. military—and had his title, won in the ring, stripped from him by fiat in 1966, as well as his licenses to box. He was not overly despondent. "No Viet Cong," he said, "ever called me 'nigger.' "

When President George Bush sent our remote-control killing machines into the red wastes of the Persian Gulf and in a few days of Operation Desert Storm they rolled up the small country of Iraq, Bush exultantly proclaimed a New World Order, saying, "By God, we've kicked the Vietnam syndrome once and for all!"

As the historian Richard Slotkin observed, Bush's gleeful pronouncement authorized "the shedding of blood . . . as a cure for the illness of our imagination."

As for Bush's New World Order, Theodore Roosevelt would have found nothing new in it.

Andrew William Mellon (1855-1937)
(National Gallery of Art)

A Vicious Class

In the 119th running of the Kentucky Derby in 1993, the bay colt Sea Hero won by 2½ lengths, a long-awaited victory for the gray-and-yellow silks of 85-year-old Paul Mellon. Paul's father, the billionaire financier and industrialist Andrew Mellon, had been Secretary of the Treasury under presidents Harding, Coolidge, and Hoover, and the ambassador to the Court of St. James in 1932-33.

The Mellon fortune had its inception in 1834 when a 20-year-old Scotch-Irish farm boy, Thomas Mellon, left his home in Poverty Point, Pennsylvania, and set off to enter Western University in Pittsburgh, 21 miles away, undecided whether to study for the law or the ministry. His parents encouraged and helped him financially through his years at school, as did his uncle Thomas, a retired merchant worth $250,000, who had made his fortune in New Orleans after the war of 1812.

The young Mellon hung out his shingle in 1839 in Pittsburgh, having decided for the law because, he said, "I could not give up my hope of bettering my condition by the acquisition of wealth." From time to time the young lawyer invested in small judgment notes or mechanics' liens if the holders of these instruments wanted their money before maturity. When he lent money on real estate, Mellon obtained a mortgage coupled with a judgment bond; when he lent money on personal security, he obtained a judgment note—that is, the debtors waived their rights. The seizing of their property was then swift and certain if they did not abide by the strictest letter of their contracts.

Thomas Mellon married in 1843—as an "alternative," he said, to continued living in a boarding house. He practiced law until 1859. His 20 years as a lawyer and investor increased his net worth to several hundreds of thousands of dollars. He had proved the truth of the couplet displayed on the office wall of a retired judge he had apprenticed to:

A pearly shell for you and me;
The oyster is the lawyer's fee.

Thomas Mellon was then elected a Pittsburgh judge and for a decade he rendered decisions and set sentences, while continuing the management of his real estate investments, particularly the Pittsburgh suburbs he was developing. He also became one of the leading coal operators in western Pennsylvania.

Judge Mellon loved land (his wife had come to the marriage with land) and coal and money and on January 2, 1870, he opened the private banking firm of T. Mellon & Sons—the sons being his two oldest, Thomas and James. The third eldest living son, Andrew William, born on March 24, 1855, was then entering Western University.

Andrew left school without graduating and at 18 with a younger brother, Richard, went into the realty and building supply business for his father. (The Judge had had all of his sons educated in a schoolhouse on his own property, by a private tutor who trained the boys in business and little else.) The panic of 1873 late in the year forced Andrew to go to work at his father's bank, where he was kept busy handling foreclosures and attending sheriff's sales to make the trifling bids that bought up properties that laboring families had sunk their lives' savings into.

In the aftermath of the panic, thousands of unemployed men roamed Pittsburgh's streets begging for food for their children and finally, in 1877, riots broke out. Railroad stations were burned, gun stores and grocery stores were looted. Troops called in from Philadelphia killed twenty of the unemployed, wounded thirty, including three children. Judge Mellon said the disturbances were caused by the "vicious classes."

His foreclosures proceeded apace and he emerged from the depression of 1880 the owner of scores of large, choice properties and coal mines, as well as the Ligonier Valley Railroad and a traction company. His unbending strictness in the matter of mortgage contracts had become legendary in Pittsburgh.

At last weary of "well doing," as he characterized his financial enterprises, Judge Mellon retired in 1885, age 71. His motto as a businessman had always been "Never go in debt." He had seldom been seen to smile. He hated taxes.

After his retirement he gave his views on the working class: "They claim a more general or equitable distribution of wealth, but disregard the prudential habits of thrift, sobriety, and self-restraint necessary to acquire it or retain it when acquired."

He gave as his opinion that "The vicious classes seem to be greatly on the increase at present, or at least show more boldness than ever before. It indicates a demoralized condition of public sentiment, which may require blood to purify."

Judge Mellon lived 23 years after he retired, his oldest and youngest sons preceding him in death. His third son, Andrew, when 22 had formed a close friendship with Henry Clay Frick, 26, after he met him at T. Mellon & Sons. Perhaps like was attracted to like: both young men were cold and imperious.

For five years Judge Mellon had been lending the youthful Frick money for his coke company. With Mellon funds, Frick bought up the distress properties of his competitors after the panic, and then raised the price of coke to iron and steel mills from 90 cents to $5 a ton. By 1879, at the age of 30, Frick was a millionaire and controlled the Connellsville supply of coal. To celebrate, he and Andrew Mellon took a tour of Europe together.

In 1880 Judge Mellon had given Andrew his power of attorney. His two eldest sons had not shown the acquisitive drive the Judge prized. Under Andrew's guidance, T. Mellon & Sons invested in loans to iron and steel works, glass factories, coal mines; it became a bank for industries.

By 1887, the iron and steel king Andrew Carnegie had become a majority stockholder in Frick's coke company. In turn, Frick had extensive holdings in Carnegie's mills, and in 1889 became chairman of Carnegie Steel. Carnegie used Frick to break strikes at the works, which Frick did superbly through starvation of the workers and intimidation by hired thugs.

In 1889 Andrew Mellon advanced funds for a new company in a new industry, the smelting of aluminum, to Charles M. Hall, who had developed the process. In exchange, he took a substantial share in and financial control of the company, the Pittsburgh Reduction plant. That same year Andrew established the Union Transfer & Trust Company to look after the estates and fortunes of Pittsburgh's wealthy. Within 10 years Union Trust was the hub of the Iron City's industrial and financial life.

In December of 1899 Frick resigned as chairman of Carnegie Steel and he and Andrew Mellon announced the formation of Union Steel to compete with Carnegie. A year later 45-year-old Andrew Mellon married Nora McMullen, the 20-year-old daughter of a Dublin distiller. Frick wired the honeymooners in London that the Mellon-Frick companies had a profit of $5 million in March. "Pretty satisfactory figures, aren't they?" Frick's telegram asked the newlyweds.

When J. P. Morgan bought out Carnegie to form U.S. Steel (and pocketed a fee of $62,500,000 for the trouble), Andrew Mellon studied the method—and then began to assemble a steel monolith of his own: blast furnaces and open hearth furnaces at Donora, contracts for cheap ore from Minnesota's Mesabi Range, a coke supply through Frick, shipbuilding yards, railroad car and locomotive foundries, bridge and structural steel plants. In order to keep its near-monopolistic position in the industry, U.S. Steel had no choice but to buy out Union Steel. In this single transaction, Andrew Mellon realized a profit that dwarfed his father's first 30 years in law and realty and coal.

Mellon's next project was to gain a monopoly of the coal mines along the Monongahela River and then of all of the coal mines in the Pittsburgh area that shipped by rail. At the mines, workers rented company houses—half a million clear profit to the company annually—and bought their food and other provisions from company stores—a million clear—small change when compared to Mellon fees for selling common stock in the combined companies or the profits on coal production from them, but money, nonetheless.

In 1902, T. Mellon & Sons, private bankers was reorganized as the Mellon National Bank. With it and Union Trust and three smaller Mellon-owned banks, Mellon now held a third of the money on deposit in all Pittsburgh banks.

Mellon lived for his vocation, lending and profiting in times of prosperity, foreclosing and profiting in times of recession. Like his father, he loved money. He never visited his company towns (called "patches"), did not concern himself with the lives of the "hunkies" who labored there. He had no interest in workers. He seldom saw his wife and he spent little time with their daughter Ailsa or son Paul. In 1910 he separated from his wife, who had been spending much of her time in England with the children.

Frail, abstemious, aloof, Andrew Mellon devoted all of his thoughts and energies to the management of coal and steel and finance—and to fashioning a 100 percent monopoly in aluminum through his Pittsburgh Reduction Company (in 1907 renamed Aluminum Co. of America). Altogether, Mellon invested only about $2 million in his aluminum properties; their growth was financed out of their profits. By 1917 Mellon's aluminum industry holdings were valued at $80 million, the market value of its stock ($20 million par) at $150 million. During World War I, Aluminum Company of America profits were 25 percent to 30 percent on invested capital. (There were charges of profiteering at the expense of the U.S. government.)

In 1893 Mellon had built an oil refinery in Pennsylvania and in 1895 he sold a Pennsylvania pipeline he owned to a subsidiary of Rockefeller's Standard Oil (at a profit of $2 million), so, when in 1900, a Texas speculator called on him to discuss the new, immensely rich Spindletop field, Mellon was not new to the profit potential of oil, and was receptive. The result was the J. M. Guffey Petroleum Company—later, renamed Gulf Oil—pipelines, storage tanks, refineries, and a foothold on the salt dome that was Spindletop. By 1920 Mellon owned 80 percent of Gulf Oil; he had started in 1900 with 40 percent. As early as 1904 Gulf

Oil was the largest independent in the world. It expanded its operations into Mexico and Venezuela.

Secrecy surrounded its financial affairs. This, it was explained, was necessary to keep greedy tax officials at a distance and to prevent Texas cotton farmers—who took a few hundred dollars a year from their fields—from becoming greedy when permission was sought to drill on their land.

Mellon divorced his wife in 1912. Nora Mellon had this to say of her marriage: "It crept over me that I . . . had been weighed coldly, dispassionately, on scales of demand and supply and as a wife ranked merely as a commodity in the great plans of this master financier's lifework. The babies were there: even the male heir was there. Was the wife to be laid off like other hired help when the steel mills shut down?"

In 1921 Mellon was 66 years old. He had spent his life almost hidden from public view in a relentless pursuit of wealth. Apparently he felt the need for public recognition of his well-doing, because when he was offered a cabinet post by President Harding, he resigned his 51 directorships and became Secretary of the Treasury. Awed by his immense wealth, newspapers throughout the country told their readers that Mellon would make the greatest Secretary of the Treasury since Alexander Hamilton.

Mellon's first recommendations were to reduce the income tax on the wealthy and repeal the excess profits tax on business. Asked what he had in mind for those with smaller incomes, he replied he had no suggestions. A slightly modified form of his recommended tax cuts was passed (and Mellon and his family saved a million dollars in taxes the first year the cuts were in effect).

President Calvin Coolidge retained Mellon as Secretary of the Treasury; in fact, Coolidge staked his campaign of 1924 on Mellon's next tax reform plan, which advocated reducing the surtax on the wealthy from 50 percent to 25 percent. Stocks boomed on Wall Street. "High rates," Mellon explained to a nation that saw him as a financial wizard, "tend to destroy individual initiative and enterprise. . . ." His plan was defeated in Congress, though the country's upper and middle classes had embraced it and Coolidge won handily.

Mellon put forward a new, more drastic tax reform plan, "The Mellon Plan," and in 1926 he stood beside Coolidge as the President signed the measure into law. If Mellon seemed pleased, it was because he could now boast that he had cut the taxes of the rich and prosperous by nearly a billion dollars and had persuaded the country to reject "socialistic tax schemes."

Q: Would you approve of them having machine guns—?
A: Such as the police here have them?

Q: I beg your pardon?
A: Such as the police have them?
Q: Well, would you approve of that?
A: It is necessary. You could not run without them.

The answers are those given in 1928 by Richard B. Mellon, Andrew's brother, who had half a century before, with Andrew, managed a realty and building supply business for their father. As the former chairman of Pittsburgh Coal Company's board of directors, Richard is responding to a Senate committee's questions about the private police system used at Mellon companies to keep their workers tractable. Richard and Andrew Mellon accepted private police as necessary and usual because they were standard in American industry—part of the "American plan" of industrial relations introduced in 1892 by Henry Clay Frick when he savagely destroyed the steel workers' union at Homestead in one of the most bitterly fought industrial disputes in U.S. labor history.

The Mellons also accepted as necessary the 12-hour day, 6-day week; it kept the "hunkies" out of brawls and brothels. They accepted as necessary wages as low as $1.75 a day and squalid company housing because they were sure that workers would not know how to appreciate anything better.

They accepted race riots as necessary. In 1917 in East St. Louis, Illinois, a strike of 2,000 workers at Mellon's Alumininum Ore Company plant made it necessary to recruit Negroes from the lower Mississippi regions as replacements—"scabs." Ten thousand responded and the company hired a few thousand.

These strikebreakers got less than the $2.40 a day they had been promised and were given box cars kept inside the works to sleep in. They were disillusioned and bitter; those who were out on strike were bitter and angry; and the thousands of southern Negroes who did not get jobs were stranded and confused.

On May 28 Negroes and whites battled on the streets. Five days later, 35,000 armed whites prowled the city's Black Belt looking for victims. A Negro woman was dragged from a streetcar by white girls and beaten almost to death. Bodies of Negro males littered the gutters; some were hanged from telephone poles; bullet-ridden bodies were thrown into creeks. The houses of Negroes were set afire and many of their occupants were burned alive in them; 310 Negro dwellings were burned to the ground. State militia were sent in and stood by while the lynchings continued. Six thousand Negroes fled East St. Louis. The strike was broken.

As Andrew Mellon had remarked when questioned about his possible guilty knowledge of the Teapot Dome scandal in Harding's administration (during which he was Secretary of the Treasury): "If you take things in this world as they are and according to your own conscience, I do not see that there is much use in getting incensed."

Until 1929 it seemed that the Treasury Secretary could have remained on the triumphant pinnacle on which he stood in 1926 after the adoption of his tax plan. He might even have aspired to the Presidency; there were rumors and trial balloons were floated. After all, he had brought permanent prosperity to the country through his management of the economy on "accepted business principles."

On October 24, 1929, however, the U.S. stock market suffered "the most disastrous decline in the biggest and broadest market of history," according to the *New York Times*. But Black Thursday was only a prelude. Four days later the market took another plunge and on Tuesday, the 29th, the loss of value of stocks on the New York stock exchange was more than twice the value of all the currency then in circulation in the United States. The bottom had fallen out with a deafening crash. Unemployment began to rise sharply, and kept rising. The Great Depression had come to America.

Mellon's New Year's greetings to the nation for 1930 concluded with: "I see nothing in the present situation that is either menacing or warrants pessimism." Privately he said that the panic of 1873 had been worse.

On May 23, 1931, he was forced to admit that his prediction of a surplus of $30 million for the nation had been wrong. Instead, the deficit for the year ending June 31, 1931, was $901 million. As the country sank deeper into the Depression, Mellon began to be attacked from all sides: There was talk in Congress of impeachment. The wizard had become the grossly inept villain.

In the dire winter of 1931-32, as the Great Depression gripped the country ever more cruelly, Mellon purchased 21 paintings from Leningrad's Hermitage Museum, paying the short-of-cash Russian government $6.1 million for them. About the same time, Governor Gifford Pinchot of Pennsylvania called on him to ask Mellon to loan the state $1 million at 4 percent interest for relief of the poor: a personal loan. Mellon declined; he felt the poor should help themselves.

On February 2, 1932, a panicky President Hoover, fearful of losing re-election because of the contempt in which his Treasury Secretary was now held, shunted Mellon to the Court of St. James in London as U.S. Ambassador to Great Britain. A congressional foe, Senator George Norris, remarked: "Picture Andy on his diminutive pipe stems in . . . knee britches in the presence of aristocracy. It does seem that the President has not treated Mr. Mellon with the respect due one of such long service."

In England Mellon repeatedly issued reassuring statements about the basic soundness of America's and the world's economy. He was sure

93

that "the onward march will be resumed." In an address in London on February 21, 1933, with 50 million Americans back home in desperate want, he said, "The economic system in America is in no danger of breaking down. . . ."

In 1932 the Mellon family fortune, bedrocked on coal, aluminum, and oil, and integrated through Union Trust (dividend rate: 200 percent annually, the highest in the world), was estimated at $2 billion. (By way of comparison, the fortune of the Rockefellers, father and son, was estimated at only $150 million in 1932.) In the 11 years of Mellon's stewardship of the Treasury Department, 9,300 U.S. banks had failed (as compared to only 2,900 from 1904 to 1920). The year after he left the Treasury, 1933, the entire U.S. banking structure collapsed. His own and his family's vast holdings, however, were unaffected.

Mellon left London on March 17, 1933, returning immediately to Pittsburgh. He died there four years later, age 82, a shrunken, very tired, discredited banker. His male heir Paul, demoralized by his parents' divorce in 1912, led a privileged if perhaps unfulfilling existence, undergoing therapy first with C. G. Jung, then later and more successfully with a Freudian analyst. His pleasures were foxhunting, collecting Impressionist paintings, and racing thoroughbreds. He lived at Rokeby's, a fine, old, 4,000-acre estate in Virginia given him by his father in an unsuccessful attempt to get him to take an interest in business. But even with all the Mellon wealth behind him, Paul had to wait 60 years, until he was 85, before a race horse he owned won the derby . . . Pity.

At the time of the divorce in 1912 Nora McMullen Mellon had said of her soon-to-be ex-husband Andrew: "Always new plans, bigger plans for new dollars, bigger dollars, dollars that robbed him and his family of the time he could have devoted more profitably to a mere 'Thank God, we are living.' "

But Andrew Mellon knew something his wife did not know: Happiness can't buy money.

A Change of Worlds

In 1855 Chief Seattle of the Dwamish tribe of the Pacific Northwest said this when he signed the treaty that doomed his people to reservation confinement:

"When the last Red Man shall have perished, and the memory of my tribe shall have become a myth among the white man, these shores will swarm with the invisible dead of my tribe, and when your childrens' children think themselves alone in the field, the store, the shop, or in the silence of the pathless woods, they will not be alone. . . . At night when the streets of your cities and villages are silent and you think them deserted, they will throng with the returning hosts that once filled them and still love this beautiful land. The White Man will never be alone.

"Let him be just and deal kindly with my people, for the dead are not powerless. Dead—I say? There is no death. Only a change of worlds."

Chief Joseph of the Nez Perce described his feelings about ownership of the earth in this way:

"The earth was created by the assistance of the sun, and it should be left as it was. . . . The country was made without lines of demarcation, and it is no man's business to divide it. . . . I see the whites all over the country gaining wealth, and see their desire to give us lands which are worthless. . . . The earth and myself are of one mind. The measure of the land and the measure of our bodies are the same. Say to us if you can say it, that you were sent by the Creative Power to talk to us. Perhaps you think the Creator sent you here to dispose of us as you see fit. If I thought you were sent by the Creator I might be induced to think you had a right to dispose of me. . . . I never said the land was mine to do with it as I chose. The one who has the right to dispose of it is the one who has created it. I claim a right to live on my land, and accord you the privilege to live on yours."

In 1744 commissioners from Maryland and Virginia negotiated a treaty with the Indians of the Six Nations at Lancaster, Pennsylvania, and invited them to send their young men to William and Mary College. The Indians politely declined the invitation—"we thank you heartily"—and countered with one of their own: ". . . to show our grateful Sense of it, if the Gentlemen of Virginia will send us a dozen of their Sons, we will take Care of their Education, instruct them in all we know, and make Men of them."

The Oglala Sioux war chief Crazy Horse, who fought against Custer and his men in 1876 at the battle of the Little Big Horn (called by the Indians "Greasy Grass"), had this view of the white man's encroachments:

"We did not ask you white men to come here. The Great Spirit gave us this country as a home. You had yours. We did not interfere with you. The Great Spirit gave us plenty of land to live on, and buffalo, deer, antelope and other game. But you have come here; you are taking my land from me; you are killing off our game, so it is hard for us to live. Now, you tell us to work for a living, but the Great Spirit did not make us to work, but to live by hunting. You white men can work if you want to. We do not interfere with you, and again you say, why do you not become civilized? We do not want your civilization! We would live as our fathers did, and their fathers before them."

In 1877 Crazy Horse was forced to surrender, placed under arrest, and then killed while trying to escape.

The Shawnee Chief Tecumseh lamented what had happened to his people:

"Where today is the Pequot? Where are the Narragansetts, the Mohawks, the Pokanoket, and many other once powerful tribes of our people? They have vanished before the avarice and the oppression of the White Man, as snow before a summer sun."

The Indian Eagle Wing told of what the Indian left behind for man to remember:

"My brothers, the Indians must always be remembered in this land. Out of our languages we have given names to many beautiful things which will always speak of us. Minnehaha will laugh of us, Seneca will shine in our image, Mississippi will murmur our woes. The broad Iowa and the rolling Dakota and the fertile Michigan will whisper our names to the sun that kisses them. The roaring Niagra, the sighing Illinois, the singing Delaware, will chant unceasingly our Dta-wa-e [Death Song]. Can it be that you and your children will hear that eternal song without a stricken heart? We have been guilty of only one sin—we have had possessions that the white man coveted. We moved away toward the setting sun; we gave up our homes to the white man.

"My brethren, among the legends of my people it is told how a chief, leading the remnant of his people, crossed a great river, and striking his tepee-stake upon the ground, exclaimed, 'A-la-ba-ma!' This in our language means 'Here we may rest!' But he saw not the future. The white man came: he and his people could not rest there; they were driven out, and in a dark swamp they were thrust down into the slime and killed. The word he so sadly spoke has given a name to one of the white man's states. There is no spot under those stars that now smile upon us, where the Indian can plant his foot and sigh 'A-la-ba-ma.' It may be that Wakanda will grant us such a place. But it seems that it will be only at His side."

Sitting Bull, a leader of the Sioux, fled to Canada after the battle of the Little Big Horn. There he was allowed to live in peace. This embarrassed the American government and a commission was sent to entreat him to return to the United States to live on an agency. Part of Sitting Bull's reply was:

"When I was a boy the Sioux owned the world; the sun rose and set on their land; they sent ten thousand men to battle. Where are the warriors today? Who slew them? Where are our lands? Who owns them? What white man can say I ever stole his land or a penny of his money? Yet, they say I am a thief. What white woman, however lonely, was ever captive or insulted by me? Yet they say I am a bad Indian. What white man has ever seen me drunk? Who has ever come to me hungry and unfed? Who has ever seen me beat my wives or abuse my children? What law have I broken? Is it wrong for me to love my own? Is it wicked for me because my skin is red? Because I am a Sioux; because I was born where my father lived; because I would die for my people and my country?

". . . Now I have said enough. You can go back. Say no more. Take your lies with you. I will stay with these people. The country we came from belonged to us; you took it from us; we will live here.''

After Custer and his troop were killed to the last man at the Little Big Horn, the Indians—who had not wanted to fight but could not escape—knew they were doomed, that the whites would take revenge. Which was why Sitting Bull led his small band of Hunkpapa Sioux to Canada.

They proved a source of embarrassment to the Canadian government, however, since the U.S. government kept raising the question of the propriety of American Indians living on Canadian soil. Forced to return to the States in 1881, Sitting Bull was unreconciled and used his great prestige with the Sioux to persuade many of them to continue refusing to sell their lands. Unarmed, he was shot and killed by Indian police in 1890 while resisting arrest.

Some few historians have suggested that the Sioux insistence on holding vast expanses of North American land, and thus denying their use to the poor of Europe, may have simply been another instance of the selfishness of the rich. . . . Of course. And a streetcar is a steamship.

About 15-20 years ago I was in northern Minnesota driving to Canada. Going to get me some walleye pike, some northerns. Lots of Ojibway (Chippewa) up there. I believe they're the only ones who can legally harvest the wild rice of Minnesota. The Mississippi River begins up there, out of Lake Itasca. You can step across it where it starts.

The Indians living up there have nothing. Their "teepees" are sometimes ragged blankets draped across a clothes line stretched between two white birches, with tin cans, old tires, dog bones, other garbage scattered around. Scrub land, stump land, sandy; too poor for growing anything except maybe Christmas trees for the Twin Cities' trade and wild blueberries and strawberries—and rutabagas, the world's worst-tasting vegetable. Mosquitoes like small buzzards and deer flies whose bite is as bad as botched surgery. Used to be a lot of iron ore up there on the Mesabi Range. No more.

Radio reception's not so good because of the little ore that's left, but I had a Canadian station coming in pretty good and the news came on late in the afternoon, the eye of the sun still low mid-sky, and one of the reports was about six Indians and the shocking thing they'd done the night before. The announcer was either stunned or outraged, I couldn't be sure which.

The paper mills up there used to use great quantities of mercury in processing pulp. Maybe they still do. There was a big mill, for instance, in International Falls, where I was going to cross over, on Rainy Lake as I remember it, most of which was in Ontario. (If you build a paper mill on a lake, you can float in your pulp logs.)

For decades the paper mills had been discharging their waste into the border lakes, and the Canadian government had recently tested for mercury in fish from the lakes and found that the level in their flesh was high enough that it was a threat to human life if eaten.

This didn't bother the resort owners around the lakes too much. They knew that three or four shore lunches of contaminated fish and half a dozen lodge meals weren't going to kill anyone and so they didn't think to mention this danger to their expense-account client/guests.

But for the Indians who lived year 'round on the lakes, fish was the staple of their diet. It was very good and very cheap—and, for them, not even that labor-intensive.

Anyway, the Canadian government had just banned the eating of these mercury-contaminated fish by Indians living in Canada. The Mounties and the local constabulary were to enforce the ban.

The Canadian radio report that afternoon said that a few days after the ban was announced a half dozen elders of one of the Canadian tribes that subsisted on the fish gathered around a campfire at lakeside and began drinking antifreeze. By morning they were all dead.

Dwight Eisenhower (1890-1969)
(Library of Congress)

Low Down, Slow Down,
Runaround Blues

The *Kansas City Star* reports that yesterday Presidential candidate
Dwight David Eisenhower declared, "I'm convinced that the Republicans
must restore true democracy to America," adding, "It is essential that
Christianity be restored in America." The *Star* also reported that "The
general, wearing a tan shirt and knit tie, beamed his famous smile."

Last week in Savannah, Georgia, according to the *Memphis
Press-Scimitar*, a young woman, 20, shot herself in a downtown bar,
leaving a note she titled "Upon My Death," directing that an airman at
Hunter Air Force Base be given her worldly goods: a 1950 Ford
automobile, a diamond ring, a check for $150, and $16 in cash. The
detective chief in Savannah said the airman "would be contacted to see
if he could disclose a reason for the shooting."

Three weeks ago T. Tom was describing the woman he'd spent
the weekend with and Dynamite Hall stopped him: "What'd you say her
name was?"

"Didn't get it," T. Tom says. "Hall maybe."

"Sounds like Darla Smith. She's a bad woman. They found a
man dead in her house couple years ago."

T. Tom looked over at Prindle and winked, Prindle blushed, but
he looked angry. Or at least upset. With Prindle it was always hard to tell
what he was thinking.

Thirty-two-year-old man in Saylervill, Kentucky, charged with
murder after "a fuss over destruction of a moonshine still," said he
"hated awful bad to kill Uncle Hag. He was a good man." Nearby to
Saylervill, a 38-year-old man got divorced on Monday. On Tuesday he
married a 44-year-old woman in Shawneetown, Illinois. On Wednesday,
shortly after 8:45 p.m., he let his new bride out of their automobile in
front of their old Kentucky home, drove to the garage, and shot himself.
His new wife said she could give no reason for his suicide. She said he

101

"looked happy."

The newspaper stories down here have a flavor of their own.

West Memphis, Arkansas, straddles the highway leading to Little Rock, directly west, across the river from Memphis. Little Rock is the capital of Arkansas, where we're headed with the cable. Memphis, of course, is the cotton capital of the world. Somebody told me that for every Southern belle in Memphis, there are two lawyers in Little Rock.

We move everything to Brinkley tomorrow, be working along the White River near De Valls Bluff. I told Mr. Clark, my Forrest City landlord, on Tuesday. He was properly regretful. Said it was a shame I wouldn't be there for duckhunting on the Languille bottoms. Limit's four in season, he said, but you go out and come back with 20 and 30 and go out again for more. "Just poor country folks," he said. "Gotta eat."

Last Sunday in the comic strips Daddy Warbucks took Little Orphan Annie out to his atomic-powered, missile-shielded yacht, which Annie had never seen. It rendered her goggle-eyed—but then everything does. She says, "But such a whopping *big* yacht! Won't it make a lot of people jealous?" to which Daddy Warbucks calmly replies, "Probably! But hardly any of the people who believe in success!"

There's a row of little business establishments on either side of the highway through West Memphis, three or four blocks of them, almost entirely Negro patrons, a couple of tourist courts, a small residential section, and some kind of factory. Might even be a whorehouse, for all I know, only here they call them "good-feelin' " houses. Plantation Club and a Cotton Club are in West Memphis, too. The Cotton Club was originally a truckers' stop, but the owner started selling beer and then he had to build an addition, the main feature of which was a dance floor with some booths and tables around it. Business got so good he had to build an addition of booths only, back of the dance floor.

The bar-keep/bouncer/door-tender is big and polite. He collects the dollar cover and stamps your hand when you step into what was originally the lunchroom and is now the "Outer Lounge & Bar."

There's dancing every night but only on Friday and Saturday nights is there a band. On these nights there's another bouncer, big and burly with a twisted left arm he can't raise to his chin, who keeps watch on the crowd from a position by the jukebox at the rear of the bandstand. Six waitresses. Mix goes for 15 cents a glass, a bowl of ice for 35 cents. You bring your own bottle or buy it from the Negro porter.

Outside is nothing but a graveled strip sufficiently wide to park two rows of cars and then the highway. But when two rows of cars are parked, the front row is trapped, so off and on through the evening the loudspeaker announces: "The owner of the cream Chevrolet, Tennessee license number 182-931, must move his car." Usually three or four such announcements have to be made before action is taken, because usually the person hemmed in is the Negro porter who runs in package whiskey whenever there's a call, and there's no hurry for him.

What light there is for this smoky cavern is furnished by 10 red-glass fixtures on the ceiling and two beer signs (the CV sign has a clock) and the colored tubing on the jukebox. The bandstand is a makeshift platform with a wooden guardrail, a middle-aged piano, a 30-year-old set of traps, and four chairs.

About nine o'clock, a big, red-haired white woman, 220 pounds, maybe, with ruffles on her dress, sits her bulk on the piano stool and begins pounding out "Blacksmith Blues," while two couples jitterbug to it on the dance floor, very free and easy, one of them a guy in red suspenders really kicking out. Place is filling up fast, and at a quarter of ten the band files in. The piano player is a stolid, balding Negro, finishing a cigar on one side of his mouth and manipulating a toothpick on the other. The leader is very short, not over five feet. He doubles on the sax and clarinet. The drummer is a small, light-skinned, lively man with a small mustache. There is a bushy-headed young Negro who plays a very sweet sax and who sings sometimes in a low, throaty voice, catching some of the tune and talking the rest of the lyrics. He sits behind the leader of the band who sits close to the guard rail and who, first thing, puts an empty cigar box on the rail.

Next to the young sax player sits another young Negro in a starched white shirt, sleeves buttoned-down, bow-tie, suspenders. The other members of the band are wearing sportshirts open at the throat. The young Negro in the white shirt and bow-tie has a very ancient, battered trumpet. He wears dark glasses and sits very straight in his chair while he plays. He is blind.

As the last jukebox tune ends (the band has been playing with it for the last half of the tune), the drummer comes down hard on the cymbal pedal and—*bang!*—the band strikes out on a tune of its own that turns the dance floor into a churning bedlam of flying arms and legs.

They play for an hour and a half before their first break. By 11:30 the cigar box is full of dollar bills and change. If you have a request, you pay or you're turned away. A lot of the requests are for pop tunes—"Honky Tonk Blues," "Botcha Me," "Married by the Bible, Divorced by the Law."

An Army sergeant comes up to the drummer and fills the tall glass he keeps at his side to within half an inch of the top with Southern Comfort. The drummer drinks and passes the glass down the line, the blind trumpeter taking it carefully from the saxman, and the music—which I had thought was already full-throttle—picks up even more.

After every number the drummer calls out, "My, my, my, it's a small world, a itty-bitty world—my, my, my!" alternated with, "Let's get together, regardless to the weather!"—invitations to put money in the cigar box.

T. Tom and Prindle are there with two women. T. Tom seems to be with this brunette, tall, a small ribbon stuck in her long hair on the left side. She is wearing a patterned dress, and smiles only occasionally. Her eyes have a sleepy cast to them and she is listening to T. Tom, lowering and raising her eyelashes to show her interest. Once she says to him, "You can go to hell for lyin' as well as stealin'."

Prindle is about 30 or so. He's pudgy, almost fat, with pock marks on his face, big nose, small eyes, and good-natured as hell. He's mixing a drink for a shorter, plainer version of the woman T. Tom is talking to. She's wearing eyeglasses and a bright red dress and she keeps smiling over at us.

They're sisters, the Smith sisters, only the one Prindle is fixing a drink for, her last name is Moore; she used to be married.

I'm dancing with the tall one later on and she's bumping up against me, batting her eyelashes, and asks me how I like the "Cattin' Club." Then after a while she says that Prindle "sure is cute, just like a li'l old sleepy raccoon," don't I think so. This is the woman Dynamite said was "bad": Darla Smith.

You had to watch you didn't get your bones broken out on the dance floor. One girl in particular flings her elbows, tosses her head, kicks her heels, rolls her belly, and flips her butt with what can only be described as wild abandon. Shirts are drenched, so are dresses. Steam rises from the crowd through the smoke up toward the red lights. The young guy in the red suspenders bridges on the dance floor, throws one leg around his partner and bends her back, and at the end of each dance bows to his audience.

About 11:30 they have to carry out the big red-headed woman who played "Blacksmith Blues" earlier. She collapses in the middle of a dance, ruffled skirt and all, done in by likker and exertion.

Couples back off from each other and then inch toward each other, bumping and grinding. When they close, they continue to roll and grind against one another for a few seconds . . . or longer.

Darla Smith has Prindle out on the floor, grinding slowly toward him, a demure half-smile on her face. When they close, the expression on his face can't be described except to say he appears to be feasting in paradise. His eyes are closed and for the first time that night Darla grins.

Once in a while a foreigner—say one of the half dozen servicemen in the bunch of singles by the bandstand—will get one of the native girls and try to jitterbug his own style with her, but this does not conform to the local mating dance and she can't follow, so she shrugs and walks off the floor. The guy in the red suspenders is all over, up and down, clicking his heels, bending over backward, nudging up close, throwing his legs out in all directions. The floor is packed, every dance, but that doesn't slow him down.

Once he has a good-looking, slightly heavy girl as his partner and she is perspiring buckets trying to keep up with him, her lids lowered as if she's in a trance, and she gets a cramp in her leg and has to stop. He tenderly walks her off the floor, apologizing profusely to the onlookers.

The band plays "In the Mood" with not two but four false stops, then "Cornbread" over and over again, each time the solos getting wilder.

One dance should, by rights, lay out the average person, but it goes on, dance after dance. The puzzling thing is that, with all the liquor, all the barely concealed invitations to rape, all the unavoidable banging into other couples, *everyone* is unfailingly, even excessively polite. You put the Cotton Club's Saturday night anyplace in the Midwest and you'd have half a dozen fights before midnight. So why the bouncers here?

About two o'clock we leave. T. Tom gets behind the driver's wheel—it's Prindle's car—and Dolores gets in beside him. Darla and Prindle and I get in the back seat. On the bridge over into Memphis, T. Tom is telling us about a town he and a buddy were in. He mutters something and Dolores says, "What, darlin'?"

"He tole me 'This is my home town. They won't hurt us,' an' he was the first one they got. *Damn!*"

We all think this over and finally Dolores takes a belt out of the bottle and reaches it back to her sister and says, "Oh, Tommie, don't be so fussy-wussy!"

Darla is snuggled up to Prindle. She takes a couple of belts herself and snuggles closer. "I'll sing, honey," I hear her say, "an' you do the huckabuck." There's room for a fourth person between me and her and Prindle.

Sunday evening I'm sitting on the front porch in Forrest City, having read the paper, cooling out and contemplating the banker's house across the street, and Dynamite pulls up in front. "They're at church," I say.

"Sleep okay last night?" he asks. I nod. "There was hell to pay," he says. "Both the wimmin got crying drunk. They was running around the halls calling out, 'Tommie, Tommie, Tommie!' and then into Prindle's room and throw themselves on his bed and cry some more. They thought T. Tom had gone off with some other woman. Cryin' *drunk!* The one says she's Darla's sister finally run up to the third floor and falls down and breaks her glasses."

"Where was T. Tom?"

"Sleeping. They was so drunk they were banging on the wrong doors."

He grimaced. "Night clerk got so upset he was making seven o'clock wake-up calls at five o'clock. I had to get the boys. The wimmin took Prindle's car an' drove off with it. They're here now, downtown. I told 'em to move on. 'I can't," Darla says, 'I'm in love with one of your crew members. 'Well, he ain't in love with *you*,' I said. 'Mr. Prindle *is* in love with me,' she says. 'We're going to be married.' "

As he's leaving, Dynamite says, "I just wanted to check up you made it back."

"Thanks," I said. "Next time you could use the phone."

After he was gone I sat there thinking about AT&T and how Dynamite Hall had spent his Sunday here tending his bosses' chicks for them and there they were way back East in White Plains devising ever-newer ways to screw him and every other one of their dedicated employees, dedicated like T. Tom and Prindle, so to say. It goes like this: They figured out that since they put in half an employee's Social Security, they can then deduct half the SS benefits from the company's pension. If the minimum, say, is $100 a month, and the retired employee gets $40 a month from Social Security, they can then deduct half the SS benefits from the company's pension. AT&T will give him $80 instead of $100, because that plus half of $40 equals the company pension of $100. If SS payments go up, AT&T's go down. As the company's slogan for all employees puts it: "No job is so important and no service so urgent that we cannot take time to perform it safely." Or cheaply, as the case always is.

Local color item in the Sunday *Memphis Press-Scimitar*: One of its staffers had a knife pulled on him in front of the courthouse in Tiptonville by the 62-year-old ex-sheriff of the county, W. C. "Peck" Haynes.

The staffer had been talking to Negroes on the courthouse lawn near a polling box, asking them if Haynes had sent them in to vote. They were Haynes' tenants. They all said yes. Reporter asked who they voted for. The response was, "How he told us." Haynes was about five yards away and the reporter took a photograph of him.

"I'll smash the camera to pieces," Haynes yelled.

"How many did you vote today?" reporter asked.

"As many as I'd a mind to. Why don't you ask them that voted? If you take another picture, I'll tear that camera to pieces."

"Are you threatening me?"

"No, by God," Haynes said, "but I will," and reached into his pocket and pulled out a knife.

Police Chief Corlis Howerton intervened. The Chief advised the reporter to get in his car and "slip quietly out of town." He said, "Feeling is high and there might be trouble. I'll follow you out of town so they won't jump you before you get out."

When they got to the highway they stopped and the reporter shook the Chief's hand and thanked him. "Haynes doesn't understand freedom of the press," the chief said, "he's been dictating so long. There was three or four of them that wanted to jump on you and I want to prevent trouble."

"The last thing I would want to do is cause bloodshed," the reporter said. Presumably with feeling.

By Tuesday Dolores was gone and on Wednesday morning Dynamite had a long talk with Prindle about his situation with Darla Smith. She was staying with Prindle but we all had our doubts if he was getting his money's worth. "What I want to know," T. Tom said to him, "is have you had carnal knowledge of that woman yet?"

"Carnal knowledge?" Prindle asks.

Me and T. Tom had a beer with Dynamite after work so he could tell us what he said to Prindle.

" 'You marry her,' I told him, 'and I'll pay you board and lodging and everything will be all right. Otherwise I don't want to see her in Brinkley or over by De Valls Bluff anywhere.'

"I wish I could tell him some of his personal business. But I can't. All I can do is run my end of it. He's 21. But she'll work him for a divorce, get his car, tie up his money, and leave him out where Christ lost his sandals."

That was yesterday. Today we got back from work, Darla was gone. So was Prindle's car. You never saw such a tragic face as Prindle's. Dynamite wanted him to get the highway patrol out after her. Prindle said no; he'd given her the car. "I felt sorry for the pore li'l thang," he said. "And now she's gone. *Jesus God!*" and he hits the wall with his fist hard as he could.

It's going to be a long, long sad trip tomorrow, moving down the line.

Was an item tonight in the *Press-Scimitar* said a Houston, Missouri, coroner's jury returned a verdict that a Negro, 27, St. Louis, died as a result of "justifiable homicide." The 79-year-old farmer who shot and killed him said he fired his .38 while the Negro was wrestling with his son, 36, near the farmhouse about dusk. All three shots struck the man, one in the head, and he died instantly.

They need those bouncers because right below the surface of all that politeness is all that rage, waiting to explode.

The VD rate in the county to which we're going is the highest in the United States—33.7. Let's hope that's per thousand. . . . Amazing, the things you can pick up reading the newspapers.

It's good to know that if General Eisenhower wins the election, true democracy and Christianity will be restored to America in this year of our Lord, 1952. . . . My, my, my!

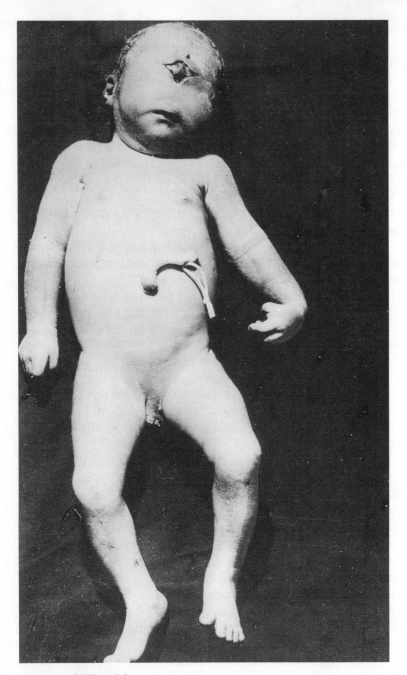

Legacy of Hiroshima.

> Mother, whose heart hung humble as a button
> On the bright splendid shroud of your son,
> Do not weep.
> War is kind.

Happier Families

. . . almost immediately after the bomb and during the following days and weeks, people began to experience, and notice in others, symptoms of a strange form of illness: nausea, vomiting, and loss of appetite; diarrhea with large amounts of blood in the stools; fever and weakness; purple spots on various parts of the body from bleeding into the skin (purpura); inflammation and ulceration of the mouth, throat, and gums (oropharyngeal lesions and gingivitis); bleeding from the mouth, gums, nose, throat, rectum, and urinary tract (hemorrhagic manifestations); loss of hair from the scalp and other parts of the body (epilation); extremely low white blood cell counts when these were taken (leucopenia); and in many cases a progressive course until death. These symptoms and fatalities aroused in the minds of the people of Hiroshima a special terror, *an image of a weapon which not only kills and destroys on a colossal scale but also leaves behind in the bodies of those exposed to it deadly influences which may emerge at any time and strike down their victims.*—R. J. Lifton, "The Theme of Death," *Daedalus,* Vol. 92, No. 3 (1963).

In 1970 the Peabody Coal Company began strip-mining 65,000 acres it had leased from the Navajo and Hopi tribes. Peabody officials gave their emphatic word that the mining would do no damage to Indian lands—would, in fact, improve the lives of the Navajo and the Hopi. Here is part of a letter that a group of unimpressed Hopi religious leaders wrote to President Nixon:

The white man, through his insensitivity to the way of Nature, has desecrated the face of Mother Earth. The white man's advanced technological capacity has occurred as a result of his lack of regard for the spiritual path and for the way of all living things. The white man's desire for material possessions and

109

power has blinded him to the pain he has caused Mother Earth by his quest for what he calls natural resources. And the path of the Great Spirit has become difficult to see by almost all men, even by many Indians who have chosen instead to follow the path of the white man. . . .

Today the sacred lands where the Hopi live are being desecrated by men who seek coal and water from our soil that they may create more power for the white man's cities. This must not be allowed to continue for if it does, Mother Nature will react in such a way that almost all men will suffer the end of life as they now know it. The Great Spirit said not to allow this to happen even as it was prophesied to our ancestors. The Great Spirit said not to take from the Earth—not to destroy living things. The Great Spirit, Massau'u, said that man was to live in Harmony and maintain a good clean land for all children to come. . . .

In May of 1955, U.S. Secretary of State John Foster Dulles gave a nationally televised report to President Dwight David Eisenhower, the two of them sitting in the President's office in the White House. Dulles told about a European trip he had just returned from, the major achievement of which was the admission of our WW II enemy, West Germany, into the North Atlantic Treaty Organization.

". . . The meeting of NATO," Dulles said to the President, "into which Germany walked in the presence of the great Chancellor Adenauer, whom you know so well and we all admire so much, walked into that room and it was a very significant and historic occasion.

". . . Adenauer himself spoke with great dignity, statesmanship. And when he had finished, the NATO ministerial council, I think for the first time in its history, burst into applause. It's a pretty stuffy formalistic body and was, as I say, I think the first time it ever happened."

Our Secretary of State went on about that historic occasion and when he was through with the subject, President Eisenhower looked him straight in the eye and said, "That was a wonderful way to tell them," congratulating him on his TV explanation to the American public, and you could just see Mr. Dulles swell with pardonable pride because he'd done his job so well. The two of them reminded me of Lum and Abner exchanging deep thoughts.

Secretary Dulles didn't take all of the credit, though. He gave part of it to Ike, which was only right. As he said to the President, ". . . you were over there effecting the liberation of Europe from our side. . . .," referring to when Ike was directing the war *against* the Germans, the Nazis, just 10 years earlier.

Well, anyway, Foster (as the President kept calling him) told about how the government of that part of Indochina (Vietnam) that we had befriended "seemed to be almost on the ropes a few weeks ago," but while he was in Europe he got it back on its feet. Then he told about going to Vienna to sign the treaty which made Austria a free country again. "Well, I said I wouldn't go to Vienna until this thing was all closed out. . . . So I planned—you gave me your plane, you know, and it was delightful, that part of it was pretty nice. . . ."

When he finally got to Vienna and signed the liberation treaty, the Austrians were really overjoyed, according to the way Secretary Dulles told the President about it: "And the older people just jumping up and down with joy, their wrinkled faces—it just made your heart feel warm at the thought. . . ." That's the way Mr. Dulles described it.

All in all, it was a very nice, folksy report the way the President and Mr. Dulles chatted back and forth. The way they talked you'd hardly have known that one was the President of the United States and the other a former Wall Street lawyer, head of Sullivan & Cromwell, a firm whose specialty is international corporate practice.

It's almost as if the two of them had been told to act like they were just plain country folk. As if some advertising man or public relations consultant had told them that an all-full-of-tears-and-flapdoodle performance would ingratiate them with viewers—and voters.

It worked. Eisenhower was so popular with the electorate that his corporate handlers even considered letting him make a few decisions on his own while he was in the White House. The lesson was not lost on politicians who followed him (it was an ancient ploy, anyway), though President Gerald Ford nearly lost it. In San Antonio in 1976, seeking to woo the predominantly Mexican-American community there—to show how down-to-earth simpatico he could be—he tried to eat a hot tamale, corn husk and all. *Muy burro americano.*

At the other pole of semantic flim-flam is the use of euphemistic jargon to conceal what is meant. For instance, we used to have a War Department but since 1947 it's been called the Defense Department.

Some other for instances: When George Bush took the country to war in the Persian Gulf, it was not called a war; it was an "armed situation." And according to our Defense Department, bombing attacks on Iraq were "efforts" and our warplanes were "force packages." Pilots on a bombing mission were "visiting a site." Buildings were "hard targets"; human beings were "soft targets." Our bombs didn't kill; they "degraded," "neutralized," "suppressed," "cleansed," "sanitized," "impacted," or "took out" targets. Killing enemy soldiers was "servicing the target."

Obviously, the Defense Department doesn't want us to know what it is doing. But how can that be? The military work for us. We pay their salaries and the billion-dollar bills for their killing toys. Why should

1930s Germany: "Train up a child in the way he should go: and when he is old, he will not depart from it."

they try to bafflegab us?

(Our ally in the Gulf War, Saudi Arabia, outdid even the Pentagon in doublespeak. As Muslims they were by religion unable to accept women soldiers from the United States, so they called them "males with female features.")

If the essence of humanity is culture—that is, the body of customs and beliefs transmitted from generation to generation (we also transmit our genes from generation to generation, but so do other animals)—and if only humans learn all of their customary behavior, and if the teaching vehicle for this learning is language, then it would seem only prudent to be careful and respectful in our use of language. Those who corrupt and debase our language are inflicting a deep, deep wound on the culture, our humanity.

The function of words is to specify, is it not? As George Orwell said: "What above all is needed, is to let the meaning choose the word, and not the other way about."

Many students of this century feel that its distinguishing feature may be man's loss of sensibility ("man" used here, and elsewhere as equivalent to the German pronoun *man*, meaning "one," a person, the equivalent, in turn, of the Latin *homo*, a member of the human species of either sex). This loss of sensibility manifests itself in incidents such as that of a woman being beaten to death while passersby ignore her cries for help and, also, on a vastly greater scale, in the murder of six million Jews by Hitler's Nazis while the rest of the world looks on.

In the furtherance of their Final Solution, the German nation attempted to exterminate the Jews. Supplanting God, the Nazis took upon themselves the right to determine who should inhabit the earth with them, the Master Race. Thus, genocide as German national policy, giving us the Holocaust, an outrage of history, just as was the bombing of Hiroshima and Nagasaki—crimes of such magnitude that the earth itself cries out.

But then what of the extermination of tens of millions of Native Americans from the time of Columbus to Wounded Knee? And what of 360 years of black slavery in North America and the scores of millions of lives crippled by that slavery? Where was man's sensibility?

In 1963 our government leaders wanted to reassure us as to our safety and security and well-being in the event our Cold War adversary, the U.S.S.R., attacked us with nuclear weapons. Of course there is no defense against such an attack, but as part of a campaign to have us believe there was, the Department of Agriculture began to issue a weekly information sheet on rural civil defense. The department's Extension Service agents took the information sheets to the editors of small-town weeklies, where they were dutifully reprinted. The handouts urged the building of fall-out shelters. They contained such statements as:

> You want to be sure of the safety of your children in school, and
> many other things. . . . Your shelter does not need to be elegant,
> it only needs to be safe. . . . Regardless of the amount of
> radiation you might be exposed to, you yourself will never
> become radioactive.

Well, yes, I'd want to be sure of the safety of my children. And,
no, my shelter doesn't need to be elegant, it only needs to be safe. And,
right, my hair may fall out, my bones and blood may become cancerous,
I may breed monsters if exposed to radiation, but no, it's true, I myself
will never become radioactive. Similarly, you don't have to live forever
to be termed immortal, but it helps.

That's to say, the weekly handouts were written for first-graders
and contained no substantive, not to say truthful, information. It was feel-
good prose written as if its readers were feeble of mind. Maybe the writer
of this childish, condescending prattle, disgusted with his assignment, set
out to satirize it. If that was the case, he did a fine job, as witness:

> Fall-out shelters to keep out dangerous radiation have been
> compared to pioneer sodhouses that protected people from hostile
> Indian arrows. . . . Even in a poorly lit shelter, children can be
> entertained with storytelling and games. If there is enough space
> and light, there could be reading, sewing, writing, handcrafts and
> other projects. Many families will want a Bible.
>
> These are only highlights. Each family will have different
> ideas and different ways to carry them out. . . . None of us could
> expect to live luxuriously under those circumstances, but we
> could expect to live and that's our aim.
>
> Protection-ready families enjoy feelings of good citizen-
> ship, strengthening our Nation's defense; and many report that
> they and their children feel more secure, more relaxed; that tests
> of shelter living bring them into closer communication and
> understanding of each other. They are happier families.

The demeaning of our language and with it the destruction of
discourse has become—amazingly—the norm in our present era of the 30-
second soundbite and the cheap shot. In 1991 Representative Newt
Gingrich, he of the quickly abrogated Contract with America, published
a booklet for the use of his fellow Republicans. It was called *Language:
A Key Mechanism of Control.* In it, Gingrich told Republicans to use
"optimistic, governing words" such as "environment, peace, freedom,
fair, flag, family, and humane" when talking about Republican policies.
"To define our opponents," the booklet advised, Republicans should use

words such as "betray, sick, pathetic, lie, liberal, hypocrisy, permissive attitude, self-serving."

Sick? Possibly. Pathetic? Slightly. Self-serving? Well, Newt Gingrich, a low-level professor in real life, has demonstrated that he mostly just runs his mouth, so you have to expect that, I suppose. The real problem is that he gives the impression that he really believes it's the whistle that pulls the train.

Newt Gingrich, and most politicians, are serious men, *Homo sapiens* whose habitat is a dark Disney World of the mind; for them the trivial is meaningful and mean-spiritedness is Realpolitik. They will do whatever is required to gain political power, including letting the word choose the meaning.

Some few years over half a century ago, the Germans liquidated the Jews of the Warsaw Ghetto. Before World War II, nearly 400,000 Jews lived in Warsaw, but by the time the Germans began their "final liquidation," only 63,000 survived. Then, against the massed might of the SS and the German Army, these survivors held out for 27 days. Here is part of the commanding German general's report on the "final" action:

> Whereas it had been possible during the first days to catch considerable numbers of Jews, who are cowards by nature, it became more and more difficult during the second half of the action to capture the bandits and Jews. . . . I therefore decided to destroy the entire Jewish residential area by setting every block afire. . . . Not infrequently, the Jews stayed in the burning buildings until, because of the heat and the fear of being burned alive, they preferred to jump down from the upper stories. . . .With their bones broken, they still tried to crawl across the street into blocks of buildings which had not yet been set on fire. . . . Frequently from the street, we could hear loud voices coming through the sewer shafts. . . . A great number of Jews who could not be counted were exterminated by blowing up sewers and dugouts.

This is the military mind functioning at its efficient, non-thinking, killing best.

The Germans have a term which expresses this trait of the military man—*Kadavergehorsam,* "the obedience of a corpse." For the Germans, obedience to your government's directives is indistinguishable from a corpse-like response. It is, for all serious Germans and all serious men of any nation, a very great virtue, one that our own government has increasingly expected of us as this present bloody century has proceeded, without sense and without sensibility.

The Hopis concluded their 1970 protest letter to President Nixon in this way:

Today almost all the prophecies have come to pass. Great roads like rivers pass across the landscape; man talks to man through the cobwebs of telephone lines; man travels along the roads in the sky in his airplanes; two great wars have been waged by those bearing the swastika or the rising sun; man is tampering with the Moon and the stars. Most men have strayed from the path shown us by the Great Spirit. . .

It is said by the Great Spirit that if a gourd of ashes is dropped upon the Earth, that many men will die and that the end of this way of life is near at hand. We interpret this as the dropping of atomic bombs on Hiroshima and Nagasaki. We do not want to see this happen to any place or any nation again. . . .

Their letter was put on file.

In his Farewell Address as President, the military hero of WW II, Dwight Eisenhower, did something he failed to do in eight years as chief executive: He warned his fellow citizens against the wiles and power of the military-industrial complex. He said that if we were not on our guard against this complex, it would lead the nation to ruin.

The people at the Pentagon thought so much of Ike's Farewell Address and of Ike himself that they had the address engraved on a metal plaque and affixed the plaque to the Pentagon where visitors could see and read it. One portion of the address had not pleased them, though; the part where Ike warned against the military-industrial complex. So they left that part out.

In January of 1996, AT&T Corporation, America's fifth largest corporation, announced it would eliminate 40,000 jobs by the end of 1998. The stock market reacted with jubilation to this news, but the working people of the country somehow saw it as yet another painful reminder that there was no job security for them, and that the future promised falling real wages and even fewer decent jobs.

The editors of the *Chicago Tribune* were anxious that their readers not sink into depression over AT&T's huge labor-force cutback. There was no reason for that, the *Tribune* editors explained. "In fact," they said,

just the opposite is true. Deregulation and an open economy have forced companies over the past two decades to become more competitive and efficient. True, it has meant job loss, retraining and loss of corporate loyalty for millions of workers, but it also has turned America into the most productive country and the best job machine in the world, ahead of Japan and Germany, who not too long ago were supposed to bury us in their dust. . . .

Eventually gains in productivity—as companies do more with less—will translate into higher wages and living standards. For now, corporations are investing record profits in new technologies and rainy-day funds, not wages and dividends. . . .

So there should be compassion for the AT&T workers, but not despair. After much gnashing of teeth over America's decline in the 1980s, the nation has regained economic vitality and a competitive edge in the early 1990s—and it will pay off, in time.

In 1968, in the *American Scholar*, Joseph Wood Krutch wrote:

I am willing to consider the possibility that we might be saved from our present perilous state by philosophy, religion, sensibility, or indeed anything that depends upon the free functioning of the human intellect and spirit. But I do not believe that we can be saved by propaganda, manipulation and conditioning. The most complete and successful application of such methods could do no more than transform us into well-behaved puppets. And that would be, not salvation, but the damnation of an eternal death.

Louis Armstrong (1900-1971)
(The Bettmann Archive)

Secular Songs

Work all week in the noonday sun;
Fifteen cents when Sat'day come.

Fer a nickel's worth of crackers and a dime's worth of cheese,
Dey treat him like a dog and do him like dey please.

I see the Captain sittin' in the shade,
YEAH, YEAH, YEAH, YEAH,
He don't do nothin' but a he gets paid.

Oh well, you kicked and stomped and beat me,
Oh well, you kicked and stomped and beat me,
Oh Captain, and you called it fun, O Lord,
O Lordy Lord.

Well, I may meet you over in Memphis,
Well, I may meet you over in Memphis,
O Captain, we're going t' have a little run, O Lord,
O Lordy Lord.

Ms. & Mr. Whitebread

In Chicago there stands a shambles of a public housing project begun in 1941, Cabrini-Green. It lies just west of Chicago's affluent Gold Coast and has 6,935 residents, nearly all of them black. Only one in 10 households in this project has an occupant who is employed. There's talk today of razing Cabrini-Green, it's in such bad shape. Maybe its residents can become boat people, live on the Chicago River nearby.

Nationwide, there are only 6.5 million low-rent housing units available for 11.2 million low-income renters who need them. This gap of 4.7 million between those who need and those who cannot find affordable housing is the widest in our 220-year history.

One of the multitude of minor scandals of the recent Reagan-Bush era in our national life (1980-92) revolved around the activities of Deborah Gore Dean, a high-ranking officer at the Department of Housing and Urban Development (HUD). It was believed that due to cronyism practiced within the department, and incompetence, fraud, and outright thievery, losses occurred at HUD during the Reagan administration that totalled from $3 billion to $4 billion.

In defense of Ms. Dean and other young Republicans at HUD accused of mismanagement and favoritism (they were called the "Brat Pack" because of their youth), it should be noted that very few in the department during the Reagan years believed wholeheartedly in the concept of federal housing programs. As they liked to phrase it, theirs was an "ideological antipathy." So if they sabotaged HUD's mandate, they were only doing what they thought was right—and having fun and dispensing favors to friends while doing it. Meanwhile, more than half of the poor of this country were spending more than half of their income on housing.

Ms. Dean was for six years a $75,000-a-year executive assistant to HUD's Secretary, Samuel J. Pierce, Jr., a former Reagan campaign aide. Ms. Dean had graduated near the bottom of her class at Georgetown

University, and had taken eight years to do it, but her political connections were first-rate. Her father was once head of the Atomic Energy Commission and her mother once lived with former Attorney General John Mitchell, the convicted Watergate felon.

One of Ms. Dean's responsibilities was to approve (or disapprove) applications in a HUD housing rehab program designed to help local housing authorities purchase and renovate buildings as low-income rentals. She okayed mostly projects reported on and developed by consultants to HUD—that is, people she know or knew of. Reagan's one-time Interior Secretary James G. Watt, for example, got $300,000 as a consultant on a Baltimore project. To earn the $300,000 he made several phone calls. The partners in a political consulting firm that worked on the Presidential campaigns of both Reagan and Bush got $326,000 for advising on a Seabrook, New Jersey, project—a project that local officials did not want. Over 15 years one of the partners is to get $15 million in rent subsidies from the unwanted project.

A former special assistant to HUD Secretary Pierce said of Ms. Dean that "She liked power. She liked the idea 'I can call the shots. I can get this for you if I want, I can stomp on you, I can kill you.' That's the kind of thing she liked."

Rising to her own defense Ms. Dean said, "I am absolutely rich, no question about it. I don't need money. My apartment in Washington is one of the nicest in town. I have a Picasso on the wall, for God's sake."

A Rockefeller or a Mellon might blink at considering Ms. Dean absolutely rich, but let it pass. She left HUD early in 1988 and the investigation into influence peddling, fraud, and thievery at HUD and her part in it began a year later. On October 26, 1993, she was convicted of 12 felony counts of defrauding the government, taking a payoff, and lying to Congress. The penalty for her offenses could have been as much as 57 years in prison and $3 million in fines. It was up to the judge.

Ms. Dean was sentenced on January 19, 1994. Despite the personal wealth in which she gloried, Ms. Dean was sentenced to 21 months in prison and fined $5,000, providing the exception that proves the rule that the high-placed and wealthy do not go to jail. I suppose she's out by now, maybe working toward an advanced degree at Georgetown, which—given her past academic record—could be a lifetime project.

At that, she can complain of sexism in her sentencing. In January of 1996 former Interior Secretary Watt was fined $5,000 and sentenced to perform 500 hours of community service and placed on probation for five years for his conduct during the same investigation that snared Ms. Dean. But no prison term for Mr. Watt, because he had erased 18 felony charges (six more than Ms. Dean's 12) by pleading guilty to a misdemeanor, acknowledging that he withheld information and documents in an attempt to mislead the federal grand jury looking into HUD.

While he was Interior Secretary during Ronald Reagan's administration Watt became newsworthy for wanting to turn public lands over to private parties, for barring the harmless Beach Boys singing group from performing on the Mall at a Fourth of July celebration in our nations' capital (he thought they might be subversive), and for describing the makeup of one Interior Department advisory panel in this way: "I have a black. I have a woman, two Jews, and a cripple." While appearing before a congressional committee, he assured the members that America need not concern itself with the possibly destructive environmental impact of his public lands policies because "I don't know how many future generations we can count on before the Lord returns."

The judge who slapped his wrist with a fine and probation said to him, "You have had a life of great integrity, and it's a shame to see what happened here." Integrity? C'mon, judge, those were 18 *felony* counts. And, hey, your honor, with all due respect, Deborah Dean's got a Picasso on the wall, for God's sake, and look what her judge gave her. James G. Watt doesn't even *like* Picasso!

"I didn't take it seriously enough," Watt said of his withholding information and documents from the federal grand jury. He added that the emotional and financial toll on his life had been "monumental." The toll on us taxpayers was pretty monumental itself, beginning with the $300,000 he took for doing nothing for HUD and going on to his misleading the grand jury that was trying to locate HUD's missing $3-$4 billion. Money not spent on low-cost housing.

Nationwide, three million U.S. citizens are homeless—in shelters or on the streets—in the course of a year. They have *no* homes to go to. As many as 40 percent of these people work full or part time, but still cannot afford even minimal housing. Families with children are the fastest growing segment of this homeless population; 22 percent of these homeless are veterans—more veterans than the number of U.S. soldiers who died in Vietnam.

But Ms. Dean of HUD did not believe wholeheartedly in the concept of federal housing programs, so there is no low-cost housing for the homeless to go to. Why should she have believed in it? She had a home—"one of the nicest in town."

When I study the careers of Ms. Dean and Mr. Watt, the things they have done and the things they have said, I am led to an inescapable conclusion: These two people are wacko. Makes you wonder how many more like them are in positions of authority calling the shots. Makes you wonder about the people who selected them for high posts in our government in the first place. And about us, who selected *those* people.

Photo by Molly Winkelman

Abuse & Abandonment

Blacks are disproportionately represented in this country in professional sports—in jazz and popular music, too—in our military, in the under- and unemployed, and in our prisons. Disproportionately, that is, meaning a far greater percentage of blacks are in these categories than in the whole population.

The United States has more blacks under arms than any other nation in the world, If the present employment differential between whites and blacks continues, we will continue to have the largest black military force in the world, almost as if U.S. blacks are hired as white America's mercenaries.

But it is in the number of blacks imprisoned that the disproportion is greatest. We pride ourselves on living in the land of the free but we perversely imprison our fellow citizens, white and black, at a rate that is far greater than anywhere else in the world, and is fast increasing. In 1995 almost three out of every 100 adult Americans were incarcerated in federal, state, and local prisons and jails (1.6 million), or on probation (3 million), or on parole (700,000). This was three times the total number under correctional supervision in 1980, just 15 years earlier. It is predicted that within a few years we will have a supervised population of more than seven million.

As for the black cohorts of this population, the statistics are even more disheartening. Half of our imprisoned are black. Add another 19 percent for Hispanics, roughly 5 percent for other minorities, and that leaves only 26 percent who are white. About three-quarters of our prison population, then, is comprised of nonwhites.

Life behind bars is brutal and nasty—unless you're a wealthy white-collar criminal or former ranking politico and are sent to one of the country club facilities maintained exclusively for your kind. In real-world prisons there is poor food, continuous boredom, fear, anger, tension, violence, and death.

"The first rule of jail is," says a guard, "the big fish eat the little fish."

Chicago street gangs control existence in Cook County Jail's Division I—a maximum-security section. Because Cook County's court system is logjammed (like most court systems in the country), many detainees, because they cannot maké bail, spend two or more years locked up in County Jail—which has 8,500 prisoners—with nothing to do all day, every day, before being tried and going on to prison and the brutal, monotonous life there.

Detainees in Division I who aren't gang members must pay gang leaders to keep from being assaulted, or having their personal items stolen, and to get access to the phones. Every kind of consumer goods, including cocaine, heroin, and marijuana, are smuggled in to gang leaders, who then sell them to other inmates at a steep profit.

Punishment is meted out for stealing, snitching, failing to pay gambling debts, or just disrespecting a gang leader. A rope of braided bed sheet is hung outside a detainee's cell to let him know that punishment is coming. When it arrives, it ranges from being punched in the head for several minutes to getting beaten with a mop handle to being slashed in the face with a razor. When a detainee is beaten so badly that his head swells, he has been "pumpkinized."

"At one point, I wanted to take the easy way out," a Division I detainee says. "But I couldn't do it. It's by the grace of God that I'm still going on."

Judges and politicians and most of us mild-mannered citizens who have not spent time in prison often regard jail rape as a normal, inconsequential extension of the criminal justice process. If, by some miscarriage of the permissiveness our society grants to whites, a white who holds to this view of jail rape is ever confronted in a byway of a building by a group of fellow prisoners whose leader says to him, "Doctor's going to have to cut you a bran' new asshole, time you get out," he would probably reconsider his position. It has been said with approximate truth that the only thing prisons positively cure is heterosexuality; 300,000 young men are raped in our prisons every year. So much for the concern for rehabilitation by a society that permits this.

There are about 90,000 women nationwide in state and federal prisons; 15 years ago there were less than 30,000. More than 43 percent of female inmates have suffered physical or sexual abuse; three-quarters of all inmates are mothers. Their 186,700 children are being raised by husbands or grandparents or are warehoused in foster homes or institutions. In Illinois, eight out of 10 imprisoned mothers are single parents.

Female inmates in Illinois who give birth in prison get only a few days with their newborn before the infant is outplaced. When you separate a mother and her child, there's not much of a family left. Even so, in the interests of budget-cutting, Congress recently eliminated an $8 million pilot project in which children under six could live with a nonviolent primary caregiver in special prison quarters. To hell with you, Congress pretty much said to the mothers: Can't do the time, don't do the crime. Get lost, Congress pretty much said to the children.

In February of 1996 the *New Yorker* magazine published an article, "Broken Sentences," by Anna Deveare Smith, who interviewed inmates and guards at The Maryland Correctional Institution for Women in Jessup, Maryland. There are about four times as many women at Jessup today as there were 20 years ago, mostly black. Here are two excerpts from Smith's interviews:

> "I have four kids out there that I have been away now for three years and I miss putting up a Christmas tree, wrapping gifts, going to the mall buying the gifts, and just seeing they face, when they open 'em up, cookin' the dinner, sittin' at the table, we all saying our grace, we all eat together, we all go visit Grandma, go over to Auntie house, and just being with my kids, I miss that."

> "I can't judge somebody else, that's what I had to learn about working in a prison. . . . I mean to me all of 'em is tragedies, especially the teen-agers. I mean high-school kids who had lives and now they have six numbers. I'm a Baptist. I believe in God and I pray. I pray for the girls every night on my knees. Yes I do. I ask him to bless everybody and let So-and So get through this time. And what I want to know is, how long is life?"

California, with its far-flung system of colleges, universities, and junior colleges, once excelled in education. Now it excels in incarceration. In the 10 years between 1984 and 1994, California's higher education system shed 8,000 jobs while its Department of Corrections hired 26,000 employees to guard 112,000 new inmates.

I have a friend serving three years in a California prison for possession of $20 worth of coke—a felony in California. That, in my opinion, is not *lex talionis*; that's *lex vindicta,* or *stupidus,* you should excuse the faulty Latin. The state of California will spend from $20,000 to $40,000 a year to keep this woman a prisoner for three years because she was caught carrying a pinch of white powder less in quantity than what Coca-Cola used to put in a barrel of the pause that refreshes.

One of three crimes committed by female offenders is drug-related. In America's increasingly ineffectual "war on drugs," in many parts of the country 90 percent of those arrested on drug charges are black in areas where blacks make up only 11 percent to 12 percent of the population. This is the Black Code in modern dress. Many state and federal sentencing statutes mandate prison sentences for *all* drug offenders, thus eliminating the option of counseling and education programs for nonviolent first-timers. More Americans are arrested for drug violations than for violent offenses, and even when charges are dropped they have thereby acquired records that can cause trouble in finding a job and in any future brushes with the law.

If pressed, most people, I think (maybe I'm wrong), would agree that confinement is too extreme a punishment for most nonviolent crimes. Especially since most nonviolent crimes are committed to support families or an addiction, and confinement does nothing to help the offender lead more productive, crime-free lives once released. There are better remedies than prison, but to find them the Unco Guid who condone the sentencing (after first defining what constitutes the crime) must ask itself how it would feel if the shoe were on their foot.

The huge sums spent to keep 5.3 million of our citizens under supervision and in prison might well be better spent on sanctions that are far less costly and much more constructive and humane. Some of these might be community service, community residential centers, intensive probation, and job-training programs relevant to the civilian labor market.

But if the white majority of this country ever decides it *really* wants to start remedying the ills of its criminal justice system, a giant first step would be the legalization of drug use. *Sixty* giant steps toward a society of law and order would be the provision to all citizens of the opportunity for a decent job at decent wages. I realize that the latter is anathema to the calculations of capitalism. I also realize that imprisoning a large percentage of the underclass may be an arrived-at-informally policy of the overclass.

California has the nation's toughest "three strikes and you're out" law, a law that means essentially that a third conviction leads to a lengthy incarceration. Nonviolent crimes represent the overwhelming majority of third-strike cases.

As a result of California's three-strike law (lobbied for by prison builders), a quarter of the regional court districts in Los Angeles County can no longer hear civil cases. Each month the county jail releases 4,200 inmates ahead of schedule because it is swamped with three-strike felons who, before the three-strike law, usually settled for a plea bargain but now demand a jury trial.

California has 30 prisons, with another four under construction. California has the third largest penal system in the world after China and the United States as a whole. It will need 15 more prisons by the end of this century; it will be a gulag in North America. The cost of its mammoth prison system will be $5.5 billion annually, about $300 per taxpayer.

In California and other states, prisoners are routinely double-celled in unnatural intimacy 24 hours a day. They serve much of their sentences sitting idly in their cells. Confined in the same circumstances, rats go berserk and eat each other, according to behavioral psychologists.

Dear Mom—You asked how I'm doing. This room, the walls are cracked, the paint is peeling, the plumbing is shot, and there's roaches *everywhere*. Flushing the toilet leaves puddles on the floor, water backs up in the sink, smells *terrible*. There's flies, mosquitoes, ants, spiders, roaches. Cigarettes cost a buck apiece if you're out. If you lose your I.D. it costs five bucks FROM THE STATE. Last night I woke up and a roach was crawling on my face. They fall from the ceiling. They're into everything, clothes, socks, toilet paper, books. They're everywhere in broad daylight. Mom, I. . . .

The war on drugs has failed; the nation's criminal justice system has become fantastically expensive and is about to founder. No matter. When you hear a crime-hawk talk show host on radio or TV or a demagogic politician ranting about getting tough on crime, the need for more prisons, longer sentences, what you are actually hearing is a call to get tough with blacks—and Latinos. Put 'em away, lock 'em away, and keep 'em away, Go to hell is the clear message. *Disappear!*

Nationwide today the number of young black males—men in their 20s—who are imprisoned or on probation or parole is one in three. By the time we reach the new century it will approach one in two. According to Jerome Miller, founder and executive director of the nonprofit Center for Institutions and Alternatives, the present system of corrections and criminal justice in the United States "is probably the single greatest contributor to crime and mayhem on the streets today." Miller has spent 30 years with the criminal justice system in one capacity or another. "For the most part," he says, "particularly in the past six to eight years, our 'war on crime' has been focused on the poor and minorities, especially black men. . . . We have succeeded in criminalizing a larger proportion of the nation, and among minority males we have given the majority a criminal label. . . . I think we will increasingly rely upon the criminal justice system as a means of managing the underclass." Miller's book *Search and Destroy: African-American Males in the Criminal Justice System* was published in 1996.

Suppose that one in every three *white* males ages 20-29 in this country was in prison, on probation, or on parole. Suppose that by the year 2001 this white-male percentage has increased to one in two; that is, half the young white males in this country, just entering the prime of their lives, will be entangled with the law. Which means that at least half the older generation of whites in this country will be the parents of criminals. It will be *their* sons who are pumpkinized, slashed with razors, and raped. And suppose that then the press and radio and TV report an epidemic of AIDS sweeping through the nation's prison system—which in 2001 has 600,000 jail rape victims a year.

A question presents itself: What would the white parents of these criminalized young white men be doing? Would they continue to live in a fantasy land where people are sharply divided between "good" and "bad"? If their children have been identified and punished as the demonic presence in our midst, would these blue-eyed, pink-toed solid citizens be screaming to high heaven for a reform of the laws, the courts, the prisons, the entire system?

Would they not.

A reform of the *entire* system—including the penalty of capital punishment.

Capital punishment—executing a human—is an exercise in sadism, vengeance, and bloodlust disguised as justice. It has been that throughout human history. It has no demonstrated effect as a deterrent.

In our society, defendants charged with killing whites are two to three to four times as likely to receive the death sentence as those killing blacks, and cases involving black defendants and white victims are more likely to result in a death sentence than any other racial combination.

Some day soon, after suitable preparation and instruction of the public, the Walt Disney Company, say, will be asked by the authorities to produce for national television a public crucifixion of a convicted criminal. It will have to be a somber show, stressing the retributive aspect of this legally approved killing, yet somehow—as only Disney can stage it—upbeat, so that we will all be able to share that combination of exhilaration, righteousness, and relief that we trust will follow the death—for good cause—of someone else, preferably a stranger.

The show, of course, will garner the highest ratings in television history. Let us hope that at the least the black who is selected for this ritual sacrifice is actually guilty.

Trespasser

In De Valls Bluff, Arkansas, they brag about the White River
fishing. The White River runs east of town and there is supposed to be
some of the best fishing in the world there: blue channel cat and bass and
bream and—for those who want them—alligator gar. Fishing for alligator
gar is done for the sport of it. You hook a gar and it comes boiling up
out of the water and fighting all the way in. It sounds and then runs at
you, gills open, and surfaces again and sounds and so on. But when it's
landed all you have is a long, heavy, ugly catch of scales. You don't
ordinarily eat gar; you do eat bass and channel cat.

Occasionally the White River crowds over its banks and floods
the low lands. It used to be that at times even the old highway into the
Bluff got flooded over. When the river subsides it leaves ponds and small
lakes behind and these hold captive fish which are easy feeding for those
gars also left behind.

The Bluff itself is situated on high ground, so its citizens don't
have to worry much about being flooded out. In fact, many of them look
forward to a flood now and again because there is less food in the ponds
left behind than in the river and, therefore, better fishing. But there are
people on the east bank of the White, the low side, who are inconveni-
enced very much by the flooding.

One old man, elderly at least, had a shack in the timber a little
over 200 yards from the east bank and every year he had a wet time of
it. In the really bad years, ever since the new highway, you could get to
his cabin by land only two or three weeks out of the fifty-two. This man,
Thomas, had been in France during World War I. When he came back
he first worked as a handyman in the Bluff. Then the Depression forced
him to move his wife and belongings out of town across the river to
government land, where living was free.

He built a house from mill scraps and next to his house he placed
an eight-foot-square tank made out of old metal road signs. He stocked

the tank with worms and went into business. Every day he sat beneath a tarp stretched between his house and the tank, waiting for customers. He developed an extraordinary sense of patience; his wife, with him.

When the old highway was still in use and a fisherman wanted a nickel's worth of worms, he turned off the highway to "Buzz's Place"—spelled BUS'S PLASE on the old man's sign.

At the bottom of the Depression, the White River, during one of its floods, threatened to change its course entirely. When it finally went down again the army engineers were called in. The engineers lined the banks with rip-rap and sank rock on mats in the river and drove pilings and after that the river held its course. Then the engineers paved a section of new highway paralleling the old on higher ground to the south and finished their project by constructing a new bridge into the Bluff.

During this construction Thomas worked 15 hours a day. Other than his service in France during World War I, it was the only steady job he ever held. When the work was completed he went back to his post in the chair under the tarp, only now—from the new highway—there was no convenient turnoff to his stand so his business dropped to almost nothing.

The next year, the Army, as a reward for its efforts in checking the river, was permitted to use the abandoned section of the old highway in a demolition exercise. Its experts buried several tons of high explosive under the old highway and moved Thomas and his wife into temporary quarters over the rear of a tavern in the Bluff and then they set off their charges. There was a loud explosion and many fish in the ponds next to the old highway were killed by the concussion, but not much real damage was done except that the reinforcing rods of the 39-year-old highway were left jutting from its surface.

When the Army left, Thomas and his wife moved back to their home. They cleaned up the litter in their yard and shored up the roof of their house, which had been left with a slight sag by the force of the explosion, and things went more or less back to normal for them. Except that now their house was completely cut off from the new highway by the snarl of reinforcing rods in the abandoned section of the old road. So Thomas got rid of almost his whole stock of worms and turned for a livelihood to turtle-trapping and fishing.

In time he and his wife became accustomed to their isolation. There life was somewhat lonely, but they were content with it and with each other. They got their food from the river, their fuel from the timber, and the occasional sale of a turtle or fish supplied the little cash they needed. They bothered no one and no one bothered them.

Their days had a careful pattern and they depended upon each other to see that this pattern was not disturbed. They arose, they worked, they ate, and they slept. They made do with their lives and they were happy enough.

When his wife died Thomas considered burying her in the river but decided against that because of the gar and the turtles. He did not take her to town and the cemetery because he could not afford to bury her there. He finally decided on a site beside the house.

He took a mattock and dug a grave for her in the center of the enclosure made by the rusting metal sheets of the old tank. He was not a young man and it took him some time to finish and when he did and had buried his wife he sat down in the chair by the tank and rested. He smoked a pipeful and then, after a time, he got up and went to the river and set the snag-line he put out every evening. When he came back to the house he went to bed.

A snag-line is a series of hooks on soft lead leaders suspended from a line. You set it up across a quiet place along the river and hope that catfish will come feeding that way. The blue channel cat feeds with an up-and-down motion as it moves along. If it runs into a hook on your line, it will give a flounce and then usually it is snagged by three or four other hooks as well. A snag-line is a fine thing if you tend it frequently enough to prevent the turtles and gar from getting to your fish. It is quite reliable.

The dry summer was very hard on the Southwest. There was no rain in some areas for as much as 80 days, and it was very hot. Around De Valls Bluff the rice farmers were sitting tight and hoping. Their hope was that their wells would carry them through, the dire possibility being that they might not. This feeling of apprehension was shared by the goldfish-farmers in the area. They raised crops of goldfish for the market just as the other farmers raised rice—with plenty of water. And water was hard to come by that summer.

Unfortunately, it was that summer in which the telephone company brought to fruition three years of planning for a coaxial cable between Memphis and Little Rock: through the conduits of Memphis, underground across Arkansas, and into the conduits of Little Rock. It was a big project and the telephone company had spent much money and hundreds of man-hours preparing for it. They did not look kindly upon the dry summer; it interfered with their operations.

The telephone company's right-of-way agents were sent out in the early spring to obtain easements. These right-of-way agents were fine fellows. If we cross your front lawn, they told you, we put down a canvas and take up the sod in rolls and put the dirt on the canvas very neatly and when we're done, every particle of dirt goes back in its proper place. Sod too.

The cable-laying itself was done by a plowtrain led by an oversize tractor upon which was mounted a giant share, two smaller caterpillars ahead on either side, pulling. The share on the big tractor ditched out an opening slightly less than a foot wide and about five feet deep. The coaxial cable was reeled out into this ditch and then the ditch was covered over by other cats and dozers. Under ordinary conditions the plowtrain was a marvel of efficiency and speed.

The other side of Forrest City the plowtrain ran into trouble. Twice it became mired for a day at a time, once in a rice field and once in a field of goldfish. The most serious delay given the train, however, was the day-to-day obstinacy of the rice farmers. This was what proved to be the most unfortunate consequence of the telephone company's bringing their plans to fruition that dry summer.

More than once it happened that the plowtrain, in going through a field, lost almost all of the field's water. Word of these local disasters spread quickly ahead of the train along its intended route and then, in spite of the fact that easements had long before been obtained by the right-of-way agents, it was not uncommon for the telephone company to be met at a fence by a farmer with a shotgun cradled across his arms.

In some cases these gun-bearing farmers had to have it explained to them many times over that the men from whom they rented the land had already legally granted the company the right to cross over the field and that therefore the train had a legal right in the field. And most of the time, in spite of these repeated explanations, the farmers would not budge out of the way.

Because it is difficult to assess the amount of damage done to a field of rice by the loss of its water in midsummer, even if that loss is only for a day, the telephone company faced with some reluctance the prospect of a multitude of claims against itself at harvest time. As a result, the plowtrain slowed to what for it was a crawl, taking extreme care of the dikes in each field that it was allowed to enter.

For several weeks the cats and dozers sat in a fallow rice field watching with mechanical indifference the herons in the next field feasting upon goldfish and frogs. The splicers behind the train were almost out of work and the General Manager in the telephone company's area headquarters in Kansas City had begun to hope for rain almost as fervently as the farmers.

When the train came to a halt, the only ditching going forward on the Memphis-to-Little Rock coaxial anywhere was just outside of De Valls Bluff in the timber next to the White River. There it was too thickly wooded, overgrown with scrub, and too uneven for the plowtrain to maneuver, and the ditching had to be let to a private contractor who worked with a dragline. So when the plowtrain was halted and its equipment left in the fallow field, the train's crew was sent to help the private contractor.

Cable had been laid across the White River, on top of the Engineers' mat, and it was the contractor's job to join this White River section with the section paralleling the new highway, which had also been placed. The contractor had to work through the snarl of the old highway as well as the underbrush and the timber and it was slow going.

The Long Lines splicing crew that worked with the plowtrain helped as much as they could, clearing away underbrush and making themselves generally useful but their hearts were not in their work. They considered it beneath them since they were all skilled cable splicers. The senior lineman—their foreman—had brought one bulldozer to the bottoms and every morning the members of the crew quarreled over the privilege of running this machine. Keeping the morale of his crew at an efficient level grew to be a burden for the telephone company's foreman.

The private contractor had his trench almost completed after three weeks' work—all but a stretch of about 60 feet, part of which was up and over the swell of ground on which Thomas had built his house. The contractor had worked his dragline without haste and dug a deep and a wide ditch. Deeper and wider than was necessary. He had worked slowly. At his own pace, that is, until the day that the management group from the General Manager's office in Kansas City came to the Bluff to look into the reasons for the delay there and everywhere else.

When the group from Kansas City arrived, the private contractor—a citizen of De Valls Bluff—proceeded even more slowly than before, because he wanted no mistake made: He considered himself his own man, and the only operator between Little Rock and Memphis who would risk his equipment in the White River bottoms, even in a dry year.

But the arrival of the management men from the General Manager's office in Kansas City did produce a flurry of activity among the train crew. They wished, naturally enough, to make a good impression upon representatives from the front office. Preceding their accelerated work tempo there was, of course, a great shaking of hands when management met labor the first morning of the visit. Management in the telephone company—as perhaps elsewhere—operates on the theory that they are part of a great team. The team theory holds that the lowliest switchboard operator in the smallest exchange in the country is no less important than is the president of the entire system himself. Management has a saying which is often repeated in its offices to the effect that One Doesn't Meet Finer People Than Those Who Work for the Telephone Company. Since management seldom meets any telephone people other than those from its offices, management considers it an important part of any field-trip task to Meet and Make Friends with the Men. Thus, the shaking of hands.

Particularly was this spirit of camaraderie shown by the senior member of the group from Kansas City, Mr. Stanton, a tall, well-built gentleman of around 45, head of the area's personnel department but being groomed for an even more responsible position in the White Plains main offices. Mr. Stanton made a special point of being friendly and

135

cordial to members of the train crew, even going so far as to pitch several spadesful of earth upon one occasion.

Before leaving Kansas City, Mr. Stanton had taken the trouble to have it ascertained for him who, among the train crew, owned stock in the company. At the river site, when the opportunity presented itself, he let it drop, man-to-man, that he also owned a few shares of stock and wasn't this delay a dirty shame. "We're all in the same boat, aren't we?" he said. "Have to watch our dividends next year if we're not careful"— this last, with a confidential, low-throated chuckle.

The men from Kansas City had made their field trip to determine at first hand the causes of delay in placing the cable. They had talked with the splicer foremen along the route, looked at maps and reports, and were concluding their investigation with a two-day stay at the White River site. By noon of their first day there, the private contractor's dragline had reached the bank of the swell on which Thomas had his cabin. Thomas had observed the approach of the dragline with interest. He had pulled his chair to a place in front of the old tank at the side of his cabin and he would sit there smoking his pipe and watching in front of and below him the huge claw of the dragline gouging away roots and dirt. He was reminded of his work for the army engineers during the Depression, and of his wife.

After lunch of the first day that the group from Kansas City was on the site, the dragline operator began to trench up the bank of the swell upon which Thomas's cabin was situated. By two o'clock he was up the barranca and there he was forced to stop. Thomas was in his chair, quietly smoking, and directly in the path of the dragline. The group from the General Manager's office was standing to one side of the cab of the dragline in conference with the foreman of the train crew. The operator called to them and pointed at Thomas. The senior member of the group, Mr. Stanton, understood the operator's gesture and clambered up the bank.

Leaning against the cabin was the faded sign from worm-selling days, BUS'S PLASE, and the senior member glanced at it as he smiled and extended his hand. "How are you, Bus?" he said "My name's Stanton. I work for the telephone company."

Thomas shook the hand and nodded, not rising from his chair in front of the abandoned tank. The dampness of the bottoms had worked upon him so that he looked and moved as if he were older and more decrepit than he actually was.

"Guess you'll have to shove over if we're going through," Mr. Stanton went on in a friendly and ingratiating tone. "Comes pretty close to your shack, I guess." He indicated the path of the ditch. "But we'll have it back-filled in no time." He waited but Thomas made no sign that he had heard.

After a silence of a minute or so, Mr. Stanton bent forward at the waist and said in a louder voice, "I guess you'll have to move, Bus. We don't want that dragline taking a chunk out of you." He laughed and slapped the elderly man on the shoulder.

Thomas looked up at him. He said, "Can you go 'round?"

The question apparently surprised Stanton because he replied somewhat sharply. He said, "We've got an easement through here. That cable can't go around, the trench has to go through. Right here." He pointed down the center of the enclosure behind Thomas's chair

Neither spoke for several moments then, and finally Stanton turned and went back down the bank to where the AT&T foreman stood. Two of the train crew had returned from the riverbank where they had been repiling rip-rap over the strip where the cable had gone into the river. They were perspiring and hot and the foreman was lighting a cigarette for one of them when Stanton came up. He related his conversation with Thomas and the foreman replied, "Well, I guess we shoot the old man and tell God he drowned."

This statement seemed to puzzle Mr. Stanton, so after a moment's further consideration the foreman volunteered that the cabin was on government land and that Thomas was, in fact, only a squatter. After making certain that his foreman knew what he was talking about, Stanton climbed back up the bank and again approached Thomas.

"Listen, Bus," he said, "we've got to go through here. You'll have to move, that's all. We're not going to hurt your cabin, just get out of the way."

But as before he received no answer. Thomas had refilled his pipe and sat smoking, relaxed, and looking levelly ahead at the dragline.

"Did you hear me?" Stanton said. "We're going through. We've been held up long enough as it is."

At this Thomas looked up and said, "If you don't mind, you'll have to go 'round." He seemed now somewhat concerned by the insistence of the man who stood over him.

Stanton turned and looked down at the foreman and the men from the train crew. He no longer tried to conceal his anger. "Couple of you men get up here and move this old buzzard," he said. "And pull out this." He pointed to the old signs which formed the enclosure that had been used for worms.

The private contractor shut off his dragline's engine and climbed down from the cab to smoke a cigarette and stretch while he waited for Thomas to move. When the foreman and the two men from the train crew started up the bank, he followed them. The other representatives from the General Manager's office in Kansas City stayed below. They were studying a chart of the White River.

When the foreman and the two crew members and the operator

had gathered around Thomas, Stanton repeated his instructions. There was then a brief period of uneasy silence because the two men from the train crew did not seem to comprehend their instructions. At last their foreman stepped forward. He grabbed Thomas by the arm. Thomas stood up slowly then, but he did not move from in front of his chair. It was clear that any man there could have moved him easily. Still, he stood there, not aggressively, but seemingly worried now.

Stanton attempted to reason with him once more, but when he received no reply he gave up and motioned to the foreman. It was then that the dragline operator intervened. The dragline operator spoke quite slowly but he kept his eyes fixed upon Stanton's face as he spoke. He said that it was almost three o'clock. He reminded Stanton that in an hour they would be quitting for the day, anyhow, and he said they might as well quit now. He said that living alone for so long had not been good for the old man and that in the morning, if they let him alone for now, he would probably be ready to move of his own accord. He said he did not believe in manhandling the elderly; it didn't look right. He suggested that they drop it for the time being, go into town, and give it a fresh start in the morning.

Mr. Stanton attempted to interrupt the dragline operator several times, and he grumbled at the suggestion that they go into town before quitting time, but in the end he gave in. Not, however, before vowing to bring the sheriff with them in the morning.

Thomas remained standing where he was until they were all out of sight. Then he went into the cabin and returned carrying his mattock, moving as if he were very weary.

When the train crew and the dragline operator and the group from Kansas City and the sheriff arrived at the site of operations the next morning, Thomas was gone. The sheriff made a short search but could not find him.

Around the enclosure next to his cabin, on the side opposite the cabin, they found a newly dug trench, about two feet deep. It started where the dragline operator had stopped his ditching the day before, skirted at right angles the rusted metal signs which formed the front of the enclosure, paralleled the side of the old tank, made another right angle turn at the rear of the tank, and picked up the original path of the ditch with another right angle.

The discovery of this trench was greeted with laughter. Then Stanton told the foreman to get going before the old man showed up again. The train crew pulled up the rusted metal sheets of the tank and the dragline operator began his day's work. In an hour and a half he had trenched across the swell of ground upon which the cabin stood.

The Little Rock-to-Memphis cable was completed in time to handle part of the heavy Christmas traffic that year. But today—many years later—there are men of the telephone company who still speak of the difficulties they encountered that dry summer.

Mr. Stanton did get the more responsible position in White Plains, where he sometimes related some of the many exasperating incidents which took place during the laying of the Little Rock-to-Memphis. He usually brought in, somewhere, the story of the detour ditch dug by the squatter. As if, as he said many times, you can bend coaxial cable at right angles.

Sometimes he injected still more humor into his narrative by quoting, drawl and all as best he could, the crew member who said of the ditch that if a snake were to urinate in it he would float away. But Mr. Stanton's many new responsibilities did not often leave him time for such tales.

In De Valls Bluff they still talk of the dry summer. And still brag about the fishing on the White River, although the year after the dry summer an eight-foot, 190-pound gar was caught at Stuttgart. This gar still holds the record for size, and Stuttgart is not even on the White River.

Sometimes in the Bluff, when the dry summer is brought up, someone will mention the cable-laying that year. Whenever this is touched upon the talk comes finally to the digging up of the woman's body next to Thomas's cabin. One who spoke to someone who was there has it for a fact that the claw sheared her in two just at the chest. They agree in the Bluff that it was a terrible thing.

But since Thomas hasn't been seen by residents of the Bluff since the afternoon of the day he stalled the dragline, indignation is usually short-lived. To change the subject, there is always the latest fishing innovation. Some of the natives go out at night now with a flashlight fastened to their boat. The goggle-eyes, in jumping at the light, flop right into the boat.

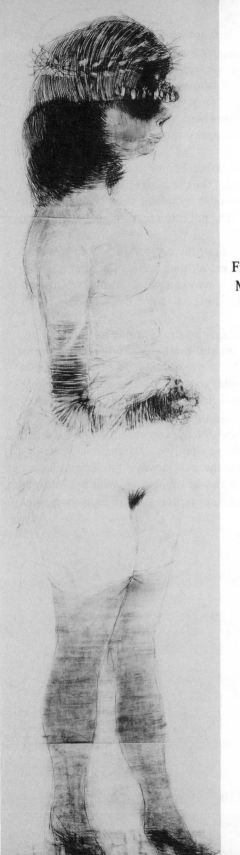

From *The Nazi Drawings* by
Mauricio Lasansky

Why You Aren't Rich . . .
and Never Will Be

Bill Gates, the presiding genius of the Microsoft computer empire, is the world's richest private citizen. His fortune in 1996 was $18 billion.

Bill Gates could cash in his Microsoft stock right now, foolishly put the money in the basement (where it would draw no interest) and every day for the next 20 years, Sundays and holidays included, spend $2 million for whatever he wanted—$2 million a day. At the end of the 20 years, Bill would still have enough left to live out his remaining years in what you and I would consider relative comfort: between $3 billion and $4 billion. (Bill's co-founder of Microsoft, Paul G. Allen, isn't that lucky; he's worth only $7.5 billion, If Paul tried spending $2 million a day, he'd be broke early on in his eleventh year.)

Or Bill could cash in and put the money out at a 6 percent return. That would give Bill over a billion dollars a year in walking-around money—forever.

Perhaps you can, but I can't, get a handle on such sums. I don't think I could spend $2 million a day for more than a few weeks without feeling a little like a spendthrift. But heck, not to worry: the chances of our ever having to do that are slim to none, and Slim's left home, we all know that.

In his book *The Road Ahead,* Bill Gates says:

> When tomorrow's powerful information machines are connected on the highway . . . you will be able to stay in touch with anyone, anywhere, who wants to stay in touch with you; to browse through any of thousands of libraries, day or night. Your misplaced or stolen camera will send you a message telling exactly where it is. You'll be able to answer your apartment intercom from your office, or answer any mail from your home.

Sure—if I've paid my electric bill. Statements like the foregoing, however, were greeted with a noisy hushed reverence by most of the nation's book reviewers. They must have been awed by that $18 billion fortune, as who wouldn't be. But they must have been asking themselves: Did he say anything?

I stay in touch with stamped letters and postcards. And, as it is, I don't see a helluva lot of citizens browsing even their local library, so where's the audience for thousands of libraries? Nor do I ever want a message from my camera, and why I'd want to answer my intercom if I wasn't in my apartment, knows only God and Bill Gates. We don't need access to information; we have a surfeit of information. What we need is access to wisdom and the compassion to use it. But I must be wrong. If Bill weren't so smart, would he be so rich?

Bill's utterances seem to me like another pitch to sell Microsoft gear and, not so incidentally, add to Bill's $18 billion. Far be it from me to be judgmental, but with the poverty there is in the world right now, isn't it a trifle sinful, if I may use that word, for anyone to have a fortune at all beyond his immediate needs and a decent provision for the future? None of us gets a special dispensation to take the surplus with us.

It was Balzac, I think, who said "Behind every great fortune there is a great crime." And Proudhon: "All property is theft." and Lee Wallek: "Past the first generation, every fortune is inherited theft, proceeds compounded."

I look forward every year to the *Chicago Tribune*'s annual round-up of Chicago's "Top 100 Companies." This year the top dog was Motorola, whose net earnings in 1995 were $1.78 billion, up 11 percent over '94.

Motorola's chief executive officer (CEO), Gary L. Tooker, received $2,041,884 in cash in 1995 and exercised $7,046,400 worth of Motorola stock options, so Mr. Tooker received a total of $9,088,284 for his efforts on behalf of Motorola in 1995.

To give you an idea of how much money that is, say Mr. Tooker works five eight-hour days a week, takes two weeks' vacation; that's more than $35,000 a day—even when he has a bad day—$4,500 an hour, $75 a minute. So every time Mr. Tooker takes five minutes to go to the restroom, empties his bladder, washes his hands, combs his hair, and straightens his tie, it costs Motorola $375. It would be a lot cheaper for Motorola to hire someone at minimum wage to go to the restroom *for* Mr. Tooker. Couple bucks, no more.

The *top* dog in compensation here in the Midwest for 1995, however, was Casey G. Cowell, CEO of U.S. Robotics Corporation, who received more than twice as much as Mr. Tooker—$18,585,858 (almost $16 million in exercised stock options), even though U.S. Robotics is a much smaller company than Motorola. (It costs U.S. Robotics almost

$800 every time Mr. Cowell adjourns to the restroom.)

U.S. Robotics' '95 earnings of $66 million were up 63 percent over '94, but that doesn't explain Mr. Cowell's huge paycheck, which is 27 percent of the corporation's profits. U.S. Robotics had a three-year total return of 756 percent on its stock (compared to Motorola's comparatively tame 122 percent return). That explains it: The board of directors was extremely pleased with that performance. They're stockholders, too.

Mr. Cowell's and Mr. Tooker's compensations were probably not all that much out of line, however. A nationwide survey of executive compensation for 305 CEOs who have been in their jobs at least since 1992 shows that average CEO pay in 1995 was 194 times the pay of the average worker. Another national survey of compensation, this time of 350 companies, found the median increase in salary and bonuses for CEOs to be 14.2 percent in 1995. In that same year, the U.S. Labor Department reported that labor costs, primarily wages and benefits, rose only 2.9 percent, just barely ahead of the 2.5 percent rise in the consumer price index. Quite often, large raises are given to CEOs because they are "downsizing" their companies, that is, firing workers—to the cheers of Wall Street.

Irene Beatriz Navarro lives in Mexico City, which with the rest of Mexico is racked by inflation. Food prices rise daily in Mexico City. Señora Navarro is 30 years old and has six children. The Navarro family lives in a cement-wall warren in a "camp"; there are thousands of these camps in Mexico's capital. When he can get work, Señora Navarro's husband earns from $7 to $14 a day. Two weeks before Christmas last year, Señora Navarro was fired from her job cleaning offices. There is a law in Mexico that requires employers to pay employees a month's wages as a Christmas bonus. Many workers in Mexico are downsized just before Christmas.

"I don't see the rich suffering," Señora Navarro says. "The rich have chauffeurs. They have nannies. They also have a cook, a washer-woman. I know, because I am all these things."

Many U.S. corporations have moved a large part of their manufacturing operations to Mexico to take advantage of the low wages paid there. When they do, they downsize their U.S. payrolls. Thus have the CEOs of U.S. corporations enthusiastically entered the global economy, especially in Pacific Rim countries, where wages are much lower even than in Mexico.

Mexican government officials frequently tell citizens that more sacrifice is needed for the good of Mexico. "How can I try harder?" Irene Navarro asks. "How? I already try as hard as I can."

In Mexico City's most expensive and luxurious nightclubs you can see the children of Mexico's multimillionaires at play into the small hours of the morning. These children spend money as if the supply is inexhaustible; perhaps for them it nearly is. They are arrogant and loud, and some of the time they seem to be enjoying themselves. They don't give the impression of having worked a day in their lives.

Señora Navarro's son is 13 years old. He works after school, which makes her feel guilty because she wishes he could spend the time studying. "People see us living like this and they think we're animals," she says. "But we love our children. We want better things."

In the Philippines, Tondo is the name of one of six squatter slums that house a quarter of Manila's six million people. The squatters live in tin and cardboard shacks on mounds of smoldering garbage and mud. The mud is infested with disease. Rats, worms, and birds fight for whatever scraps of food come with the garbage that is dumped at Tondo every day.

There is no running water or electricity in Tondo. Its human residents scramble for food, for tin cans, for bottles, anything they can find in each day's garbage haul that can be eaten or sold.

A century ago the United States liberated Manila and the rest of the Philippines from Spanish rule, and the islands became a market for American goods and a source of raw materials for the U.S. economy. Today, the residents of Manila's Tondo can buy almost nothing and they produce nothing. American CEOs have written them off as consumers. They no longer exist except as animals. This is executive-level triage, that is, corporate decisions as to who is worthy to inhabit the earth, and who is unworthy of notice—or food.

In our own country, the richest in the world, 25 million Americans—one in every 10—beg at food pantries and soup kitchens. One of every three children in this country lives in poverty. This is not a temporary condition and it is worsening. There will be, perhaps there already have been, discussions at the highest executive levels about triage for America's workforce.

Rich as we are, we have become a low-wage, low-employment country. In industrialized countries, the United States has the largest gap between its rich and its poor. These are the fruits of unrestrained monopoly capitalism or, rather, government-subsidized monopoly capitalism.

When a company changes hands or merges with another, the surplus executives have million-dollar golden parachutes but its workers who lose their jobs go hungry. (Man can adjust to almost anything except not eating.)

The accepted rule of thumb for the black jobless rate is twice that for whites; if you're black, get back. The Hispanic jobless rate used to be 1½ times that of whites; now it's approaching that of blacks. Minorities are also far less likely to get managerial or executive-level positions. The U.S. economy excels at nothing so much as producing poorly paid and unemployed workers.

Say you are the single-parent mother of Michael, four, and Caitlin, two. Four mornings a week you rise at five o'clock to go to work in a CPA's office. For three of those days you are his secretary and receptionist. For two days a week you work a shift at a supermarket. On Saturdays you arise at six to go into the CPA's office to clean it and catch up on the week's overload of typing and filing. Your employer could afford to hire you full-time, probably should, given the work load. But then he would have to provide benefits. This way, you're a temp and he's excused. You've heard the one about the CPA who didn't know all the angles? . . . Neither has anybody else.

Say you are a woman working in a hotel, cleaning your allotment of rooms—vacuuming, making beds, washing out bathrooms, room after room, day after day for $800 a month. Well, the laborer's worthy of her hire, they say. But it isn't like that in the real world. There, it's: Chicken one day, feathers the next.

Your job is keyboarding legalese for a law firm. When a client's merger is nearing the point of last hammering out, overtime is mandatory. You have Carpal Tunnel Syndrome but you live with the numbness and the pain and pray that your condition does not get so bad that you cannot work. You have no medical coverage: Your job is freelance. Once in a while you get the elevator, most of the time you get the shaft.

Say you are a man who runs with a large, wheeled cart from house to house in the Chicago suburbs, five days a week, in the heat of July and August and in the biting cold of January, picking up trash and garbage and trundling it out to the street to dump into a waiting garbage hauler—that you also drive along the route. Always at the run. Do you know what stamina is? Fatigue? Exhaustion? Do you spend a lot of time in the evenings or on weekends browsing thousands of libraries on the Internet?

Say that you are the parents of nine children. You live in Texas but each year you take your family to Michigan to harvest fruits and vegetables, sunup to sundown, living—the 11 of you—in a two-room wooden hut for the season. It's a wonderful life.

Long ago, *Life* magazine ran a photo of migrant workers harvesting sugar beets in Minnesota. The caption read: "Mexicans do not mind bending or working in the hot sun." *Life* would not print such a caption today; it would not be politically correct. But *Life* today might classify you and your family as being of the "working poor." What would be more accurate to say is that you are poorly paid.

We have a global economy now at the end of this century. What is meant is that capital will establish its plants anywhere on the globe where there is the cheapest labor. Two dollars and twenty cents a day in Indonesia means no jobs at all in Akron, Ohio. The 20 percent of the world's population who live in the richest countries of the world receive 82 percent of the world's total income at present. The poorest 20 percent survive—barely—on 1.4 percent. But all this will change, is changing. Eventually, poverty will have spread over the globe uniformly and the richest countries in the world won't be quite so rich anymore; the poorest, not quite so poor—but workers in every country will still be underpaid, as close to the starvation level as is possible to maintain and still keep the requisite number functioning. And the rich will be even more immensely wealthy.

The world today has 350 billionaires whose combined net worth equals the annual income of the poorest 45 percent of the world's entire population. The very wealthy of the United States and the world have no sense of national interest; they have no concern, much less feel any sense of obligation, however slight, to anyone who has less than they do. Theirs is a stateless alliance that defines the profit objectives of a global economy as identical to their personal gain. In 1961 Octavio Paz wrote:

> The "advanced" nations reply very calmly that it is all a matter of "natural economic laws" over which human beings have very little control. . . . Actually, of course, the law they are talking about is the law of the lion's share.

Let us call the very wealthy of this country our "overclass." For the last 20 years at least, some would say the last 200, for reasons of ever greater profits only, our overclass has waged war against working people. Corporation profits today are at record heights, and productivity increases annually, yet workers' real wages continue to fall, both in recessions and recoveries. Job security for most Americans is almost nonexistent. Workers are laid off before they become eligible for pensions; pension funds are raided by corporations, that is, stolen.

What does a corporation's head man, its CEO, do to earn his millions? Well, he attends a lot of meetings, dictates a lot of letters, delegates a lot of tasks, works long hours (I hope Motorola's Tooker puts in more than the 40-hour week I credited him with), and he makes decisions. The last is the most important part of his job. If his decisions seem to work out favorably 51 percent of the time, he is a managerial genius.

Don't let this get around, but with just a little luck, you or I could be managerial geniuses simply by flipping a coin every time there was a decision to make. That's the way honestly flipping a coin works out. You could look up the statistics.

For the record, the average compensation of the CEOs of Chicago's Top 100 Companies in 1995 was $1.79 million. No one deserves that kind of money for flipping a coin. Or anything else. Here are the names, companies, and total compensations of the Midwest's top five CEOs in 1995:

Casey G. Cowell	U.S. Robotics	$18,585,858
Floyd L. English	Andrew Corp.	17,317,903
John N. Brincat	Mercury Finance	12,952,690
Gary L. Tooker	Motorola	9,088,284
Arthur M. Goldberg	Bally Entertainment	6,203,812

This was their direct compensation. As CEOs they also got a bundle of perks, starting with company jets and limousines.

The immense annual windfalls of these men—and Bill Gates no doubt puts them all in a long shadow—are one big reason why you aren't rich. Or, worse, don't even have a job.

The main reason you're never going to *be* rich, however, is that you're not a member of the dwindling (in numbers) of the overclass; you're a member of the dwindling middle class or the burgeoning underclass. What you should know is that when you play the game of life and you lose every time, all the time, the game is rigged. As Malcolm X said, "If you see somebody winning all the time, he isn't gambling, he's cheating."

It should be noted that stock options given to CEOs are not necessarily tied to performance. In 1995, William Smithburg, CEO of Quaker Oats (cash compensation: $1,033,055), was awarded a stock option grant of $8.6 million, even though Quaker Oats, trying unsuccessfully to peddle Snapple to the public, had a very embarrassing year. You see, CEOs commonly sit on the boards of directors of each other's corporations, and one hand washes the other. We are living in the Gelded Age.

Lastly, please note that John W. Madigan, in the ninth spot for Midwest top earners in 1995 ($2,978,814), is CEO of Tribune Company. The *Chicago Tribune* has a fat, lively, and informative daily and Sunday Business Section. It has no Labor Section at all.

Coda

When I graduated from high school I enlisted in the Navy to see the world. I saw San Diego and San Francisco. When I was discharged from the regular Navy I signed on for six years with the reserve and then enrolled in the University of Iowa, determined to graduate in four years (because that's how long my GI Bill ran), no matter how long it took.

Six months or so before graduating, in the fall of 1951, I went to Washington, D.C., to test and be interviewed for employment with the Central Intelligence Agency, an organization that back then nobody knew much about. At one of the interviews, a professor of history from Princeton asked me to discuss German colonies in Africa before WW I, one of many subjects about which I was ignorant. I tapdanced for about three minutes and when I finished, my Ivy League interrogator told me that the Germans had never had any colonies in Africa. I still think he was wrong, but I didn't look it up back then and I'll' be damned if I will now.

At another interview, a CIA officer told me that as part of the overall indoctrination there would be paratrooper training at Ft. Benning. "You'll be thrown in with a low class of people," he said. "You may not like some of them." I guess he thought he was talking to one of John Jacob Astor's great grandsons.

The CIA accepted me and told me to enroll in a course in spoken German at the university (*Wo ist der bahnhof, bitte?*), because my assignment was Berlin! I would own an electronics store; that would be my "cover." There would be a powerful transmitter hidden in the basement of the store and when the Russians rolled into Western Europe, occupying all of Berlin, I would radio out reports from behind enemy lines as to what they were really up to. I could see a few flaws in this scenario, but what did I know about intelligence-gathering?

Then I made a mistake. I went to the university library and sought out an article on paratrooper training; there was one in *Collier's* magazine. I remember standing there in the stacks, sweat suddenly starting to run down my ribs when I came to a photo taken from the plane's jump-off hatch, looking down thousands and thousands of feet. But by the time I finished reading the article—in horrified fascination—I had squared my shoulders and faced up to it. Without question, I was chicken.

Finally I phoned the recruiter at the CIA and called it off. By then, though, there was only a month to graduation, and I had no job waiting. After frantic scrambling around, I was hired by AT&T Long Lines as an "executive trainee" ($70 a week), not something I'd probably otherwise have chosen. That was how I wound up in Arkansas working with telephone craftsmen—that was a part of the year-long Long Lines' training program. (Forrest City, where I spent a few weeks, has fallen on real hard times. To help, the federal government is building—this year, 1996—a prison outside of town.)

We also had classes in Kansas City and then we moved to Chicago. I lasted six months before I was cut line to line ("downsized"). There were no doubt many incidents that brought about this early check to my high hopes for a business career but I like to think it was a question I asked deliberately, knowing its answer, in Kansas City. One day we trainees were being conducted through the Long Lines switching center there—row after row of female operators patching thousands of long-distance calls every second, and every operator lily-white, whereas the Kansas City I knew outside the building we were in had a *large* Negro population. So when the success-oriented middle-level executive who was conducting our tour asked if we had any questions, I asked him why there were no Negro operators. He sort of waved one hand, and our tour continued.

They fired me in Chicago on New Year's Eve day. After the success-oriented executive who had the termination assignment gave me the bad news, he asked his secretary—a beautiful Polish girl who looked a little like Kim Novak (and whom, it was somehow commonly known, the exec was banging) (the secretary, not Kim Novak)—to bring him some forms that were needed and then we sat there. He squirmed a little, moved the photo of his family an inch to the right, moved my personnel folder closer to himself, opened it, scanned the top sheet, looked across his desk at me. "I see," he said, after first clearing his throat, "that you were an English major."

Great, I thought; we need small talk right now. I nodded.

"Did you," he said, clearing his throat again, "did you take any other languages?"

After AT&T severed me (without severance pay), there were 40 years of this job and that job, mostly scutwork, but a lot of it very satisfying, and now I'm retired and living on my Social Security supplemented by freelance work.

I live in a suburb of Chicago, the same suburb that Michael Jordan of the Chicago Bulls basketball team lives in, as a matter of fact. I've never seen him out here, though. (I did see Scottie Pippen once, at the Jewel Food Store. We were in the same otherwise empty aisle, not three feet from each other! I said, "Way to go, man!" and he looked at my white-maned head as if it was empty.)

Jordan and I live in different parts of town. His house cost two or three million dollars, and mine didn't. We also have different interests, another reason we haven't met. For example, he likes to play golf, and I don't, though, truth to tell, none of the country clubs up here would let the world's greatest basketball player join, anyway. Even if he wanted to.

Looking back on my years of gainful employment, can I offer the youth of this great nation any advice? Yes. When you are discharged from the Navy, don't go to college. Get a job with the post office, if you can. Over the long run, the hours, pay, benefits, job security, and retirement program will probably prove immeasurably better than can be found elsewhere in the economy.

In grade school and high school I was taught that the United States had never lost a war. The clear implication was that we were always victorious because our cause was always just.

In all of my Minneapolis grade-school classrooms there was either a portrait of Washington or of Lincoln at the front of the room. We were told that Lincoln had first understood and felt the iniquity of slavery at a slave auction in New Orleans, to which he'd traveled down the Mississippi as a young man.

In my bedroom at home my parents had hung a reproduction of a painting of Sir Galahad (by G. F. Watts) when I was a year old. It was still there when I left for the Navy, having subtly influenced my choices in life, possibly. My father worked for Ralston-Purina, which sponsored the radio adventures of that straightest of straight-shooters, Tom Mix. I grew up thinking hard work does it, honesty is the best policy, and merit will be recognized. That had worked for my father. He had graduated from high school and gone on to become a Purina vice-president.

My family on both sides going back to the old countries—Germany and Sweden—were farmers and laborers. My grandparents went through terribly tough times in the late 19th and early 20th centuries in the Midwest, but they all thought this country was great. So did I. Perfect, is what I thought, and I felt very lucky to have been born here, a land with liberty and justice and opportunity for all. I believed this, even growing up during the Depression.

This information is given because despite any impression to the contrary gathered from this book, I would like to be thought of as a citizen who loves his country. My parents lived the American Dream, and I believe in it—as a dream, let the ambiguity stand.

At any rate, there you have that much, though I'm not sure it's helpful. Because my younger brother has the same genes that I do and essentially the same background, and politically he's a rabid fan of Rush Limbaugh and I can't say that I am. So possibly neither nature nor nurture figures as importantly in what we become as we are sometimes told they do. (An evolutionary biologist could explain it, maybe.)

When 500 years ago the Spaniards came to conquer the New World they proclaimed they were going to do it for riches and for God, in that order. These past mid-months of 1966, as I write this and the Presidential campaigns crank up, there have been a great many fund-raising dinners for the candidates, dinners attended by the very wealthy as guests of honor because they have it to give. Here is a typical invocation at one of these dinners, spoken by a man of God, of course, in this instance the Reverend Stanley Mast, of the LaGrave Avenue (Detroit) Christian Reform Church:

> "O God, as we gather together tonight to honor important people in our country, we pause to acknowledge that you are master of the universe and Lord of the nations. As we focus on finances and politics, we give you thanks for the gift of wealth, we thank you for the privilege of living in America, this great land of freedom, a land that not only allows but even encourages the individual pursuit of wealth. We thank you, O God, for the success so many of us have had in that pursuit. . . . Bless our guests of honor. May their generosity and faith inspire us all. Bless these upcoming elections. May the right people be elected. And God bless America. Amen."

There's so much just religiously wrong with this invocation that to criticize it would almost be worth casting the first stone. But I quote it only to demonstrate that there is very little difference between the 16th-century Conquistadores and us. This has become a land dedicated solely to the gathering of riches by a righteous, ruthless few. I don't think that's why America was once known as the last best hope of the world.

In a predator-economy such as we have, we know where such single-minded devotion to greed leaves most of us: with *their* foot on *our* necks. Life is rude enough and strange and full of sorrows enough without that. The overclass seems to have a deep need to hate (their fear turned inside out) and fiercely protect and add to what they have, at whatever cost to the rest of us. Compassion and cooperation do not figure

152

in their equations, not to mention love. If they can define those who have less as unworthy, as different from themselves, they can shut their eyes to any amount of suffering and want. (If slaughterhouses had glass walls, most people would probably become vegetarians; most, *but not all.*) Perhaps the Manicheans had it right: The fate of the world *is* in doubt and the forces of evil may yet triumph. What is certain is that it is capitalism that incubates and nurtures the greed and hatred and fear that cripple our society.

Very little I've written in this book was taught me in the classrooms upon which Washington and Lincoln looked down. I think, probably, it's not being widely taught today, if at all. Yet it is part of our history, and accounts in great part for where we are today.

Racism is, has been, will continue to be a product of capitalism. The racism of slavery was, as well, of course. All of the ugliness of racism will increasingly be used against a wider and wider spectrum of people, against everyone who has nothing by those who are increasingly approaching more closely to having everything.

The rich have their own, very destructive addiction: wealth. There is no 12-step program for this addiction, and those who have it will lie, cheat, steal, and kill for it. They do, every day. We could become a completely color-free society, and still have a small, greedy, governing overclass addicted to wealth and a huge, governed and exploited underclass—just as long as the rules in force today still obtain.

Lincoln said: "Slavery is founded on the selfishness of man's nature—opposition to it in his love of justice. These principles are in eternal antagonism; and when brought into collision . . ., shocks and throes and convulsions must ceaselessly follow." He also said: "As labor is the common burden of our race, so the effort of some to shift their share of the burden onto the shoulders of others is the great durable curse of the race." Those statements summarize what this book is about, or at least that was the intention. The consequences of our situation, our predicament, as well as its solution, if there is to be one, seem to me implicit.

When you treat other men and women and children—whatever their color—as if they were not human, when you do this to get what *you* want, at their expense, as if they had no right to inhabit the earth on the same terms as you do, that defines *obscene.*

"Indeed, I tremble for my country when I reflect that God is just."—Jefferson.

The students who in 1957-58 integrated the 1,950-member student body of Little Rock's Central High School: front row, left to right—Thelma Mothershed, Elizabeth Eckford, Melba Pattillo; back row, left to right—Jefferson Thomas, Ernest Green, Minnijean Brown, Carlotta Walls, Terrence Roberts, Gloria Ray. (UPI/Corbis-Bettmann)

"In Ole Virginny": happy, happy antebellum plantation times as depicted in *Harper's New Monthly Magazine*, **June, 1876.**

CUTTING HIS OLD ASSOCIATES.

AN OF COLOR. "Ugh! Get out. I ain't one ob you no more. *I'se a Man, I is!*"

Harper's Weekly, January 17, 1863

KORN-KINKS

malted corn-flakes ready to serve

Kornelia Kinks

"Ain't he a likely pickaninny? That's what comes from eatin' co'n. Co'n fed folks is cheerful. They is always up an' doin'. You've no idea how much good eatin' they is in a package of Ko'n Kinks until you try it. It's good for the fambly and for every one in the fambly."

— *Kornelia Kinks.*

5c. Korn-Kinks, the new food, corn and malt, to be eaten cold or hot, for breakfast and all meals. For sale at all grocery stores. 5c. a package.

The H-O Co., Buffalo, N. Y.

Good Housekeeping, advertisement, February, 1907

From *Oh Skin-nay! The Days of Real Sport* **(1913) by Briggs, a widely popular book of drawings celebrating the simple, youthful pleasures of "all us fellers."**

Jim Crow. (Detail from a poster by Alan Crosland for the Warner Brothers movie *The Jazz Singer*, 1927.)

Photo by Stanton Kramer

Two from muddled America. (Drawing by R. Crumb)

Rest and rehabilitation. (Drawing by R. Crumb)

The dispossessed.

Sitting Bull (ca. 1834-1890)
(Mercaldo Archives)

Chief Joseph (ca. 1840-1904)
(Dictionary of American Portraits)

The dispossessors. (*McClure's Magazine*, July, 1899)

A home in Mexico City (Azteca Stadium in background).

Otto Rene Castillo / 1936-1967

APOLITICAL INTELLECTUALS

from *Camels Coming*: 1967
San Francisco
Editor: Richard Morris

One day
the apolitical
intellectuals
of my country
will be interrogated
by the simplest
of our people.

They will be asked
what they did
when their nation died out
slowly,
like a sweet fire,
small and alone.

No one will ask them
about their dress,
their long siestas
after lunch,
no one will want to know
about their sterile combats
with 'the idea
of the nothing'
no one will care about
their higher financial learning.
They won't be questioned
on Greek mythology,
or regarding their self-disgust
when someone within them
begins to die
the coward's death.

They'll be asked nothing
about their absurd
justifications,
born in the shadow
of the total lie.

On that day
the simple men will come.
Those who had no place
in the books and poems
of the apolitical intellectuals,
but daily delivered
their bread and milk,
their tortillas and eggs,
those who mended their clothes,
those who drove their cars,
who cared for their dogs and gardens
and worked for them,
                         and they'll ask:

"What did you do when the poor
suffered, when tenderness
and life
burned out in them?"

Apolitical intellectuals
of my sweet country,
you will not be able to answer.

A vulture of silence
will eat your gut.
Your own misery
will pick at your soul.
And you'll be mute,
                         in your shame.

translated by Margaret Randall

Curt Johnson was born in Minneapolis and attended the public schools there, high school in Iowa Falls, Iowa. After serving in the Navy, he attended the State University of Iowa. He has lived in Chicago for the past 45 years, earning his living as an editor.

Other Titles from December Press That May Be of Interest—

The Otis Ferguson Reader . . . "For students of Depression culture, jazz history, or prose style, this book is indispensable."—*Serials Review* . . . 327 pp., $12.50

The Mafia Manager: A Guide to Success, by Lee Wallek . . . 160 pp., $10.00

The Dillinger Dossier, by Jay Robert Nash. Speculation that the FBI killed the wrong man in 1934 . . . 273 pp., $15.00

Song for Three Voices, a novel, set in contemporary Chicago, by Curt Johnson . . . 220 pp., $10.00

Young in Illinois, stories and essays by Robert Wilson . . . 112 pp., $8.00

Order from December Press, Box 302, Highland Park, IL 60035. Add $1.50 for postage.